HIRE THE BEST
...and Avoid the Rest

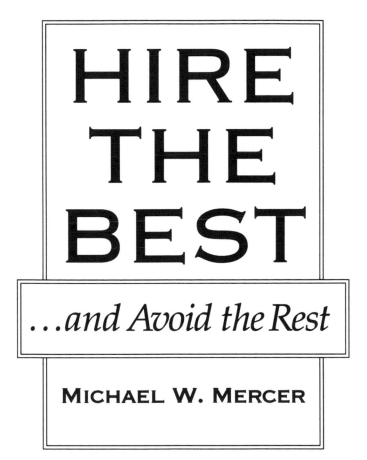

HIRE THE BEST

...and Avoid the Rest

MICHAEL W. MERCER

American Management Association
New York • Atlanta • Boston • Chicago • Kansas City • San Francisco • Washington, D.C.
Brussels • Toronto • Mexico City

This book is available at a special
discount when ordered in bulk quantities.
For information, contact Special Sales Department,
AMACOM, a division of American Management Association,
135 West 50th Street, New York, NY 10020.

This publication is designed to provide accurate and authoritative information in regard to the subject matter covered. It is sold with the
understanding that the publisher is not engaged in rendering legal,
accounting, or other professional service. If legal advice or other expert assistance is required, the services of a competent professional
person should be sought.

Mercer, Michael W., 1950–
    Hire the best . . . and avoid the rest / Michael W. Mercer.
        p.   cm.
    Includes bibliographical references and index.
    ISBN 0–8144–0207–0 :
    1.   Employee selection.   2. Personality and occupation.
    3.   Prediction of occupational success.   I. Title.
    HF5549.5.S38M47   1993
658.3'112   dc20   93–2512
                                                                    CIP

Printing number

10 9 8 7 6 5 4 3 2 1

To the memory of
my wonderful friend
Vincent J. McNamara

Contents

Preface

A captivating, though unverified, quotation goes like this:

> "Every single day, millions of workers are idle. Fortunately, almost all of them have jobs!"

Did you ever hire any of those people? Unfortunately, all too many managers, executives, and business owners have not only hired such unproductive and undependable people, but they often *still* have some on the payroll!

Profits derive from a work force composed of productive, dependable, and honest employees. You can get this kind of work force by hiring people who possess the required *job-related:*

1. Behaviors
   - Interpersonal skills
   - Personality traits
   - Motivations
2. Mental abilities
   - Reasoning or problem-solving skills
   - Computation skills
   - Verbal skills, including spelling, grammar, and appropriate word usage (especially necessary in employees who write or type/word-process memos, letters, and reports)
   - Ability to handle work requirements, such as small details, with speed and accuracy
3. Character
   - Work ethic
   - Honesty
   - Freedom from substance abuse
4. Technical skills
5. Specific job-related knowledge

Most important, the *purpose of evaluating job candidates is to predict—or forecast—how they will perform on the job before they are added to the payroll.* However, research and experience show that most managers are woefully inept at predicting how well candidates will do on the job.

Fortunately, such prediction skills are easy to acquire—when managers are shown simple, quick, organized ways of learning them.

That is exactly what this book aims to show you. I've taught thousands of managers in a wide array of companies and a broad range of industries how to interview and test job candidates and how to conduct useful reference checks.

They invariably feel excited by their newfound skill in *accurately and easily* evaluating job applicants. These managers appear to have had a burden lifted from their shoulders. They look relieved and express more confidence in their ability to pinpoint which candidates are most likely to turn out top-notch—and which would be only average or below-average.

I also receive eye-opening calls from managers who took my "Hire the Best . . . and Avoid the Rest" workshops and consultations. They convey two interesting types of information: (1) They tell me which of the candidate evaluation skills I taught are helping them to hire high achievers; and (2) they tell me how they hired one or two underachievers when they strayed from the candidate evaluation techniques I had instructed them to use.

Based on these insights from managers whose hiring decisions affect their ultimate success or failure, I found out what works for a broad spectrum of managers, executives, and business owners. This book shows you how to do it right the first time and every time you evaluate applicants so that you can always hire the best.

This book also helps you to hire candidates purely on the basis of their potential to do the job rather than on the basis of any nonjob-related biases you may have. Doing so will not only square you with the spirit of the employment laws. It will also enable you to uncover which applicants really are most likely to produce outstanding job performances. This will help organizations and job candidates in three ways.

1. Managers can lead more productive work groups. Why? They hired the best person to do the job regardless of the employee's nonjob-related background.
2. Companies can boost their profits and productivity. Such benefits grow out of hiring the best, again regardless of nonjob-related factors.
3. Everyone gets a chance to compete on merit rather than on the basis of genetic or cultural factors. Winners in every field of human endeavor, in effect, belong to a meritocracy of high achievers who hone their skills to do highly productive, valuable work.

Every high achiever takes his or her raw materials and crafts them into vital work talents. Such people tackle their jobs with gusto. They know what to do. They combine their motivations, intelligence, and social skills to figure out how to succeed and stand out. In the outcome, they help their careers and bank accounts.

Each one of these high achievers also sets an example of excellence—to co-workers, friends, and family—and becomes a role model from whom others can learn how to succeed and come out on top in their careers.

Another unique and highly useful service this book provides is its presentation of how to test job candidates. A review I did of books on evaluating job candidates revealed a startling fact: *None* of those books showed how to test applicants.

This void keeps managers from hiring the best. Why? There is abundant research indicating that the most accurate way of predicting a candidate's on-the-job success is through the use of valid, reliable preemployment tests.

For this reason, I show you step-by-step ways to use preemployment tests. As an industrial psychologist, I spent over four years doing in-depth validation research to develop these two tests. Companies across North America now benefit from using them. They are:

1. The Behavior Forecaster
2. The Abilities Forecaster

My numerous experiences in helping managers to choose and properly use preemployment tests have taught me how to explain how to use tests simply to predict candidates' actual job success. Readers receive the benefit of my expertise in test development and use in Chapters 4 and 5, which are devoted to making preemployment tests easy to understand and useful for all managers.

Finally, I discovered in my workshops and consultations that as managers learned how to accurately predict candidates' potential to succeed on the job, they then faced a new puzzle: How should they put it all together? That is, how could they combine their candidate evaluations from the three methods—interviews, tests, and reference checks—so as to lead to the wisest hiring decisions?

To resolve this predicament, I developed the Candidate Rating Sheet. This form uses arrows to graphically display predictions about each candidate. Using the Candidate Rating Sheet, as shown in Exhibit P-1, boils down to making job offers only to those applicants who get "up" arrows on all candidate evaluation methods.

This arrow technique works wonders! For instance, when I teach this arrow technique to managers, I almost invariably see a light go on. Suddenly, they possess a graphic, easy-to-use tool with which to make their crucial hiring decisions. Most managers relate better to the visual arrow ratings than they do to verbal ratings (such as poor to excellent) or number ratings (for instance, a scale of 1 to 3 or 1 to 5). You, the reader, learn how

Exhibit P-1.   Arrow candidate evaluation sheet for a candidate who is likely to succeed on the job.

Candidate Evaluation Method	Arrow Rating
Interviews	↑
Tests	↑
Reference checks	↑

Note: "Up" arrows indicate judgments made on the basis of the candidate evaluation method predicting that the candidate will do well on the job.

to use this creative, highly practical arrow technique throughout this book.

All in all, I am delighted to show you ways to *accurately, easily,* and fairly *quickly* predict how each candidate will actually perform on the job. These methods really work! By putting this book's how-to techniques into action in your hiring procedures, you could hire the best . . . and avoid the rest.

Michael W. Mercer
Chicago, Illinois

Acknowledgments

I want to thank the following people for their help, advice, suggestions, and encouragement: George Arteaga of Westburne Supply, Inc.; William C. Byham, Ph.D., of Development Dimensions International; Paul Cherrier of Spohn, Cherrier & Associates; Robert Cormack of Personnel Systems Corporation; Robert Hoffman of The HR Assignments Group; John Hunter, Ph.D., Michigan State University; Dale Kerkman of Dale Kerkman & Associates; George A. Lisenbe of Management Evolvement Inc.; Alan S. MacLean of Western Carolina Industries; Jeffrey M. Mercer, Esq., of the Law Offices of Jeffrey M. Mercer, P.C.; Henry Paquin of Q Technologies Incorporated; David Spohn of Spohn, Cherrier & Associates; J. D. Thorne, Esq., of Petrie & Stocking; and Joseph E. Troiani, Ph.D., of Community Psychiatric Centers, Inc.

Especially affectionate thanks go to Dr. Maryann Victoria Troiani for her vibrant enthusiasm for my business endeavors and adventures.

Adrienne Hickey of AMACOM deserves special appreciation for a number of reasons. To begin with, she "discovered" me. A number of years ago, Adrienne heard me deliver a speech to a ballroom packed with managers. She approached me, handed me her business card, and asked me about the possibility of writing a book on the topic of my speech. I felt like one of those legendary movie stars discovered by a talent scout. I did write the book, and AMACOM published it. The book is *Turning Your Human Resources Department Into a Profit Center*. Writing and speaking about this book across North America tremendously expanded my career and allowed me to help thousands of managers both to increase their companies' profits and to enhance their careers. I will forever feel grateful to Adrienne. This book,

Hire the Best . . . and Avoid the Rest, is the second I have written with Adrienne as my senior editor. I feel incredibly proud that AMACOM is again serving as my publisher.

I thank Mike Sivilli of AMACOM, who served as associate editor for this book. His upbeat spirit and fast-paced approach made it a joy to work with him.

Also, I appreciate Erica Buneo, senior editorial assistant at AMACOM, for doing a great job helping Mike Sivilli in making sure the editing of the the book went smoothly and that the typeset galleys looked sharp.

Finally, a special thank-you goes to my family: my mother and father, Rhea and Philip; my sister and brother, Meridith and Jeffrey; and my aunt, Idelle. They taught me two crucial lessons about life: (1) that I can accomplish practically anything if I persist in working at it, and (2) that a positive mental attitude not only generates more fun, it is also a delightful way to live life each day.

1

Introducing How to Hire the Best . . . and Avoid the Rest

In the course of the many speeches I deliver and the management workshops I conduct, I often pose this question to listeners or participants:

> "What's the fastest, cheapest, easiest way to have a work force composed of productive, dependable, and honest employees?"

The responses always prove well-meaning yet rather off the mark. For instance, most managers suggest that there should be better managers and supervisors to direct employees, that work force training should be increased, or that attitude surveys should be conducted to uncover what stands in the way of employees doing a good job.

They almost all miss the most effective way of quickly, cheaply, and easily obtaining employees who are productive, dependable, and honest. The real answer is the following:

> "Hire people who are productive, dependable, and honest!!"

The first and absolutely necessary step in assembling a topnotch group of employees is to hire people who are highly likely to perform well on the job. That's it! Absolutely no other method works as effectively.

Companies can get fantastic managers, provide current employees with the greatest training programs, and remove innumerable obstacles that hinder employees' productivity. But all these wonderful techniques will undoubtedly work much better when the employees themselves are productive, dependable, and honest to begin with. Such people make all the other well-meaning—perhaps even magnificent—programs and management techniques successful. After all, the best management-sponsored processes and procedures always produce the best results when employees with a penchant for success are involved.

The Goal of Evaluating Job Candidates

The key goal of evaluating or assessing job candidates is to *predict—or forecast—how applicants will perform on the job* before *they are hired.*

After all, wouldn't a sharp manager prefer to know how likely it is that a person will succeed *before* hiring that person? Isn't that vastly more useful than finding out the truth after the person is on the company's payroll?

All the prediction methods presented in this book zero in on specific techniques that will help every manager accurately predict how each candidate will perform on the job if hired. Using these techniques greatly increases the probability that a manager will hire the best . . . and avoid the rest.

The Costs of Hiring Below-Average or Only Average Employees

Managers always wonder how well they have predicted an applicant's aptitudes or abilities for the job they were hired to fill. And they often feel let down when, months later, they find out that they may not have hired the most productive, dependable, or honest employee.

How long does it take for a manager to discover how effectively a new employee performs on the job? To help answer this question, I surveyed many managers from a wide array of organizations as to the amount of time it takes to judge the competency level of a new employee in executing his or her job. The essential results appear in Exhibit 1-1.

In general, the fewer the skills required to do the job, the more quickly a manager can determine if a good hiring decision was made. The more skilled or complex the job, the longer it will take to discover if a worthwhile candidate was chosen for the position.

Exhibit 1-1. Length of time it takes managers to evaluate a new employee's effectiveness on the job.

Type of New Employee	Months Needed to Evaluate New Employee's Effectiveness	Average Monthly Salary and Benefits	Amount of Salary and Benefits Spent
Unskilled or semi-skilled employee (e.g., untrained or barely trained production worker, entry-level clerical staff	1–2 months	$1,280	$1,280–$2,560
Skilled employee (e.g., secretary, bookkeeper)	3–6 months	$2,000	$6,000–$12,000
Professional (e.g., accountant, engineer, salesperson, computer programmer)	4–8 months	$3,200	$12,800–$25,600
Manager	6–12 months	$5,333	$31,998–$63,996
Executive	12–24 months	$133,000	$133,000–$266,000

Note:
1. Average monthly salary is based on the following hourly pay guidelines: Unskilled or semiskilled employee—$6; skilled employee—$10; professional—$15; manager—$25; executive—$50
2. Calculations are rounded off to make the exhibit easier to read.
3. Benefits are computed at 33 percent of salary. Thus, the benefits of an employee earning $6/hour are $2/hour.

Of course, the potential salary and benefits figures shown in Exhibit 1-1 do not take into account "lost opportunity" dollar amounts. For instance, if a company hires a highly productive salesperson, he or she will produce more sales dollars than an average or below-average salesperson—sometimes a lot more. But a less-than-fully-productive manager or executive could cost a company tens of thousands or even millions of dollars in expenses or lost profits. That is the lost opportunity cost of not hiring a first-class manager or executive, who could help add a huge amount to a company's bottom line.

More about the cost-benefits of hiring productive, dependable, and honest employees is presented in Chapter 7.

All in all, the important points to remember are that a manager who hires above-average to excellent employees will have a more valuable work force, and that a manager who hires only average or below-average employees will end up paying lots of money for lower productivity and profits. Therefore, it always *pays* to hire the best.

Lost opportunity costs are not the only costs you could be shackled with as the result of hiring below-average employees. If you are eventually forced to fire a nonproductive, unreliable, or dishonest employee, you may find yourself hauled into court.

According to a study reported in the prestigious *Stanford Law Review,* a company is much more likely to be sued for terminating an employee than for not hiring an applicant.[1] In fact, more than six times as many lawsuits are brought for termination than are brought for not hiring in the first instance.

Obviously, a company is more likely to avoid litigation when it hires productive employees who do not have to be terminated. On top of that, these above-average or excellent employees:

- Help increase profits.
- Help reduce costs.
- Obtain the high productivity needed to keep the organization financially healthy and growing.
- Set good examples for the company's work force.

The stakes are, in fact, huge. Hiring worthwhile employees is the key to work force productivity, productive use of time and people, and the avoidance of termination-related lawsuits for under-performance. Given these crucial, bottom-line concerns, a manager really needs a scientific crystal ball to predict how a candidate will perform on the job if the manager hires that person. There are three main methods for making such predictions. Each can be used to increase the likelihood that only winners are hired.

Methods for Predicting Candidate Success on the Job

The three key methods managers use to evaluate job candidates are the following:

1. Interviews
2. Tests
3. Reference checks

Although managers will recognize these three methods, most managers are far from expert at putting them into action to hire the best. The different chapters in this book explain practical, step-by-step ways of using each method as a kind of crystal ball to predict ultimate on-the-job success.

Characteristics of Useful Prediction Methods

All candidate prediction methods that make useful forecasts concerning the candidate's future success on the job have four characteristics in common. They are:

1. Job-related
2. Valid
3. Reliable
4. Used by the company in a nondiscriminatory manner

First, a *job-related* prediction method means that the interviews, tests, or reference checks are concerned with the knowledge, skills, and abilities needed to succeed in the specific job to be filled. For instance, the job-related criteria for a secretarial job would differ substantially from those for a managerial job. The secretary's job-related criteria might include typing, filing, and answering the phone. The manager's job-related criteria might include planning, delegating, and conducting meetings. Certainly, some of the secretary's and manager's job duties may overlap—for example, both may need to maintain good customer service—but many of the qualities sought in a secretarial candidate would be unnecessary in a managerial candidate, and vice versa.

Second, a *valid* prediction method means that the interviews, tests, or reference checks accurately predict what they claim to predict. For example, if a key attribute needed to succeed on a job is teamwork, then the interviews, tests, or reference checks used to assess the candidate must accurately or validly predict how teamwork-oriented the candidate really is.

Third, a *reliable* prediction method provides dependable results. To illustrate reliability by its opposite, consider an experience most managers have had at one time or another: Two managers both interview the same job applicant. They then sit down together to discuss the applicant. As each, in turn, gives his or her impressions of the candidate, they sound as if they are talking about two different applicants. These two managers arrived at differing conclusions about the same applicant's potential on-the-job performance! That is an example of an *un-reliable* interview. Research shows that most unstructured interviews (i.e., when interviewers ask whatever questions pop into their heads rather than set questions) are woefully unreliable.

By contrast, if two managers both score a test taken by the same applicant, they both will arrive at the exact same test scores. Why? The test scoring is objective and, as such, inherently more reliable.

Fourth, the company should use its interviews, tests, or reference checks in a *nondiscriminatory* way. That is, the company should not use the prediction methods for the purpose of discriminating against people on the basis of their (1) genetic makeup—for example, gender, age, or race—or (2) nonjob-related disabilities.

Characteristics of Legally Justifiable Prediction Methods

Legally permitted candidate screening methods have four characteristics.[2] They are:

1. Job-related
2. Valid
3. Reliable
4. Used by the company in a nondiscriminatory manner

Isn't that amazing? Legally permissible prediction methods have the exact same characteristics as useful candidate prediction methods!

Actually, this makes very good sense: The underlying rationale of employment laws is to insist that organizations base their hirings, promotions, or terminations on whether employees really can or cannot do the job. In this regard, interviews, tests, or reference checks should delve into whether or not a candidate can carry out *job-related* duties. This should be predicted on the basis of methods—such as interviews, tests, or reference checks—that can be shown to be *valid* and *reliable*. And, of course, the company must use these prediction methods in a *nondiscriminatory manner.*

Predictive Validity of the Three Main Prediction Methods

Since the goal of evaluating job candidates is to validly predict how well each candidate will perform his or her job-related duties, what does the research tell us about the three methods? Key research results appear in Exhibit 1–2, which shows that tests are the best predictors of future job performance.

To understand the predictive validity research presented in Exhibit 1-2, it is necessary to understand that the numbers shown there are *correlations, not percentages.* Correlations range from −1.00 all the way up to +1.00. The higher the correlation, the more two factors go together. For instance, there would be a high, positive correlation (approaching 1.00) for the link between height and weight. Why? Because, in general, the taller someone is, the more that person weighs.

A correlation of .00 means that no correlation exists between two factors. For example, a company could flip a coin to predict which applicant will succeed on the job. Such a method would yield a .00 correlation with actual job performance, since it would turn out correct half the time and wrong the other half.

Exhibit 1-2.   Predictive validity of methods used to forecast candidates' actual job performance.

Prediction Method	Predictive Validity Correlations
Interviews	.14
Tests	
Ability tests	.53
Personality tests	.38
Reference Checks	.26

Sources: John E. Hunter and Ronda F. Hunter, "Validity and Utility of Alternative Predictors of Job Performance," *Psychological Bulletin*, Vol. 96, No. 1, 1984, p. 90; Robert P. Tett, Douglas N. Jackson, and Mitchell Rothstein, "Personality Measures as Predictors of Job Performance: A Meta-Analytical Review," *Personnel Psychology*, Winter 1991, p. 703.

Given this baseline of .00, the higher the prediction method's correlation with actual job performance, the better that method forecasts a candidate's job performance.

The results show that most *interviews* result in inaccurate predictions of job performance in that the correlation is only .14. That is because most interviewers do not know how to interview and/or how to make valid or accurate predictions based on their interviews. However, all is not lost for interviews. Structured interviews prove much more accurate at predicting actual on-the-job performance than the usual ad hoc, unstructured interviews. Chapters 2 and 3 show readers how to plan and conduct structured job interviews.

In sharp contrast to most interviews, *tests* do well at correctly predicting job performance. Ability tests, such as intelligence-related questionnaires, show a high validity of .53. Personality tests premised on the personality traits needed by the job holder also provide good predictions of actual on-the-job behavior, with the validity correlation at .38. Chapters 4 and 5 teach readers how to use tests to help make on-target evaluations of job candidates.

Finally, reference checks generally do not provide accurate predictions of how a candidate will do on the job. After all, their predictive validity correlation is only .26 in the classic study cited in Exhibit 1-2. However, since that research was conducted, there has been widespread concern that someone giving a negative reference about a job seeker might be sued for defamation or invasion of privacy.[3] Given this apprehension, many companies today refuse to discuss applicants' actual job performance when prospective employers inquire. Because of this development, the validity of reference checks may now be even lower. Chapter 6 shows readers ways of obtaining references despite the intense anxiety companies feel about discussing their former employees' job performance.

Combining Data From Interviews, Tests, and Reference Checks

What's a manager to do? To begin with, most managers have a hard enough time just interviewing. Next, it is becoming increasingly difficult to get valid reference checks. Finally, how can managers add tests to their recipe for predicting applicants' ultimate job success?

It is simple using the *arrow method*. Imagine arrows denoting the following:

- An up-pointing arrow, ↑, pointing toward 12 o'clock, indicates a prediction that the candidate will do well on the job.
- A sideways-pointing arrow, →, pointing toward 3 o'clock, means a prediction that the applicant will be only average on the job.
- A down-pointing arrow, ↓, pointing toward 6 o'clock, signifies a prediction that the candidate's job performance will be bad.

Using the arrow method, a company should show a preference for hiring applicants who have only up-pointing arrows, as shown in Exhibit 1-3, on all their interviews, tests, and reference checks.

Interestingly, about 80 percent of the questions I receive from companies using my preemployment tests or interview skills training revolve around what to do with candidates who get all up-pointing arrows *except* for one down-pointing arrow.

Exhibit 1-3.   Arrow technique predicting how successful a candidate will be on the job.

Applicant Evaluation Method	Top Candidate	Average Candidate	Below-Average Candidate	Poor Candidate
Interviews	↑	→	↑	↓
Tests.	↑	→	→	↓
Reference Checks	↑	→	↓	↓

My answer always is the following: Go find candidates who earn *all* up-pointing arrows. Find applicants with a great likelihood of turning into high achievers on the job. Avoid average or below-average candidates like the plague.

Notes

1. John J. Donohue III and Peter Siegelman, "The Changing Nature of Employment Discrimination Litigation," *Stanford Law Review,* May 1991, pp. 993–1037.
2. J. D. Thorne and Michael W. Mercer. "Legal Rules and Bottom Line Reasons for Pre-Employment Testing," *Die Casting Engineer,* March/April, 1993, pp. 50–51.
3. Art Durity. "Time for a Reference Check-Up," *Personnel,* December 1990, p. 1; and Kenneth L. Sovereign, "Pitfalls of Withholding Reference Information," *Personnel Journal,* March 1990, pp. 116–22.

2

Interviews for Forecasting a Candidate's Success on the Job

Part I: How to Quickly Pinpoint Candidate Talents to Look for and Simplify Note Taking

Interviewing is the most widely used method for evaluating job candidates. With few exceptions, almost every job is filled on the basis of interviews.

Interviewing entails doing the seven key steps shown in Exhibit 2-1. This chapter shows how to do Steps 1–3. Chapter 3 explains how to carry out the remaining steps.

Job Analysis Checklist: A Fast Way to Pinpoint What Candidate Talents to Look for in Each Interview

Interviewers invariably wonder: "What should I look for in this interview? What are the key make-or-break job-related criteria an applicant needs to succeed in this job?"

Exhibit 2-2 walks you through the process of selecting what specifically to look for in each interview. It lists key job-related criteria that could be useful in a wide variety of positions. Prior

(text continues on page 15)

Exhibit 2-1.   Steps in the interviewing process.

1:   Do job analysis using Job Analysis Checklist.
2:   Design Interview Guide Form for each specific job.
3:   Give a copy of the Interview Guide Form to each interviewer.
4:   Interview each candidate, using mainly open-ended questions while taking careful notes on the Interview Guide Form.
5:   Give arrow rating (up, down, or sideways) to each candidate.
6:   Discuss each candidate in a meeting of all interviewers.
7:   Fill in Candidate Rating Sheet.

Exhibit 2-2.   Job Analysis Checklist for pinpointing job-related criteria an applicant must meet to succeed in each specific job.

Directions
Step 1:   List the job title for which you are using this checklist.
Step 2:   Check *all* the job-related criteria an applicant must meet to succeed in the job listed in Step 1.
Step 3:   Narrow down the list of job-related criteria checked in Step 2 to the most crucial six to nine, make-or-break job-related criteria.

CANDIDATE FOR (fill in job title): _____

Job-Related Criteria	*Behaviors Related to Criteria*
NONCOGNITIVE JOB-RELATED CRITERIA	
Interpersonal Skills	
_____ Friendliness	Is outgoing, warm, shy, withdrawn
_____ Assertiveness	Is passive, assertive, aggressive
_____ Prefers working solo	Likes working alone
_____ Prefers teamwork	Likes working in groups
_____ Verbal skills	Explains things clearly and uses words well
_____ Persuasiveness	Sways others' opinions and actions
_____ Tact	Is mannerly and diplomatic
_____ Candidness	Discusses problems and raises questions

Personality Traits

_____ Persistence   Is tenacious, persevering, oriented toward long term

_____ Creativity   Is innovative on the job

_____ Follows rules and procedures   Works "by the book"

_____ Handles obstacles well   Bounces back easily and is emotionally objective

_____ Optimism   Focuses on opportunities and solutions

_____ High energy   Seems tireless, busy, animated

_____ Focus on feelings   Emphasizes emotions, personal relations

_____ Focus on facts   Emphasizes basics, how to get things done

_____ Poise under pressure   Handles stress well

_____ Being a self-starter   Is a self-starter, does not need others to organize project

Motivations

_____ Being achievement-oriented   Often mentions goal achievement

_____ Desire for high earnings   Emphasizes earning $

_____ Desire to help people   Likes serving and assisting people

_____ Desire to do creative work   Enjoys innovative work

_____ Desire for power   Enjoys taking charge, controlling

_____ Desire to increase knowledge   Enjoys doing research

Management and Leadership Skills

_____ Planning skills   Makes plans for one or more years

_____ Organizing skills   Makes sure work is done in a logical way

_____ Delegating and controlling skills   Assigns tasks to subordinates, follows up on delegated work to make sure it is done right and on time

(continues)

Exhibit 2-2   *(continued)*

_____ Skills in motivating others	Sparks morale and productivity

Job-Related Criteria	*Behaviors Related to Criteria*

COGNITIVE JOB-RELATED CRITERIA

Technical Job Knowledge and Skills

_____ Knowledge of _____ *(fill in)*	Possesses specific job knowledge
_____ Skill in doing _____ *(fill in)*	Can put knowledge into action on the job

Note: Many skills can be tested by means of work simulations or assessment center exercises, as explained in Chapter 5.

Thinking Techniques

_____ Organized thinking	Is logical, systematic, uses lists
_____ Detail-focused thinking	Sees individual trees, not just the forest
_____ Whole-picture thinking	Doesn't lose sight of the forest because of all the trees
_____ Objectivity in decision making	Bases decisions on research rather than on gut feelings or intuition
_____ Intuitive decision making	Relies more on gut feelings than research to reach decisions

Mental Abilities

Note: Mental abilities are evaluated mainly on the basis of tests, since such abilities are hard to pinpoint in a job interview.
_____ Reasoning/problem-solving ability
_____ Vocabulary ability
_____ Computations/arithmetic ability
_____ Grammar, spelling, and correct word usage
_____ Ability to handle details with speed and accuracy

to each interview, you—or other managers familiar with the job in question—can use this Job Analysis Checklist to pinpoint the make-or-break criteria the candidate must meet to succeed in the job. Use this checklist *before* designing the easily customized Interview Guide Form, which is explained later in this chapter.

The criteria in the *Job Analysis Checklist* include four noncognitive and three cognitive categories:

Noncognitive Job-Related Criteria

1. Interpersonal skills
2. Personality traits
3. Motivations
4. Management and leadership talents

Cognitive Job-Related Criteria

1. Mental abilities
2. Thinking techniques
3. Technical knowledge and skills

Examples of the top six to nine job-related criteria are shown in Exhibits 2-3, 2-4, and 2-5 for the positions of salesperson, secretary, and manager, respectively. The criteria listed are appropriate for the organization that selected them; the criteria for success in these positions in other organizations may differ.

Exhibit 2-3. Job-related criteria for a salesperson's job.

Assertiveness
Prefers working solo
Persuasiveness
Handles obstacles well
Optimism
High energy
Being a self-starter
Desire for high earnings

Exhibit 2-4.   Job-related criteria for a secretarial job.

Friendliness
Persistence
Follows rules and procedures
Optimism
Poise under pressure
Desire to help people
Knowledge of computer programs:
XYZ Word Processing and ABC Spreadsheet programs
Organized thinking

What to Look for in Interviews: Sample Questions to Ask for Each Job-Related Criterion

Armed with the six to nine most important job-related criteria for a particular job, listed in Exhibit 2-2, you can now proceed to the next most important task in preparing to interview job candidates. This task entails quickly customizing an Interview Guide Form on which to take notes during the job interview and insert your ratings after the interview. But before creating the customized Interview Guide Form for a job opening, it may be useful to scrutinize all the job-related criteria in terms of how to spot each criterion during the interview and the questions to ask the candidate to extract information regarding each job-related criterion.

Exhibit 2-6 will help you greatly in these two matters. To begin with, it lists the same job-related criteria shown in brief in

Exhibit 2-5.   Job-related criteria for a managerial job.

Prefers teamwork
Persuasiveness
Optimism
Desire for power
Planning skills
Delegating and controlling skills
Detail-focused thinking
Objectivity in decision making

(text continues on page 33)

Exhibit 2-6.   Job-related criteria: What to look for in interviewing candidates and sample questions to ask.

NONCOGNITIVE JOB-RELATED CRITERIA

Interpersonal Skills
Job-Related Criterion: Friendliness
What to Look for in Interview
   Candidate's comments to listen for:
   - Enjoys socializing.
   - Looks forward to being around people.
   - Likes doing things with friends.

   Nonverbal actions to watch for:
   - Creates good first impression.
   - Smiles readily.
   - Exudes warmth.
   - Is outgoing.
   - Is gregarious.

Sample Questions to Ask
   "What aspects of your last job appealed to you most?"
   "What activities did you enjoy carrying out?"
   "What activities did you least enjoy carrying out?"
   "What have been your biggest problems in working with people?"

Job-Related Criterion: Assertiveness
What to Look for in Interview
   Candidate's comments to listen for:
   - Takes charge of projects or tasks.
   - Follows up repeatedly.
   - Pushes herself into situations to make an impact.

   Nonverbal actions to watch for:
   - Leans forward when interviewer disagrees.
   - Is passive in interview situation.
   - Is assertive in interview situation.
   - Is aggressive in interview situation.

Sample Questions to Ask
   "Describe how you handled participating in a committee or task force."
   "Give me specific examples of what you did when prospects or customers did not call back."
   "When you've worked on a project with others, what specifically did you do to get the project completed?"

(continues)

Exhibit 2-6   *(continued)*

"Tell me about a time when you knew someone was not being as efficient as possible in doing his or her work. What did you do?"

Job-Related Criterion: Prefers Working Solo or Prefers Teamwork
What to Look for in Interview
  Candidate's comments to listen for:
    ▪ Enjoys working alone.
    ▪ Enjoys working in groups.
    ▪ Bothered by people who slow down work or who make mistakes.
    ▪ Likes collaborating.
  Nonverbal actions to watch for:
    ▪ Displays emotional facial expressions when talking about working with others.
Sample Questions to Ask
  "Tell me how you prefer to carry out projects."
  "What was the most exciting project you ever did on that job?"
  "Describe some projects you had to do but later wished you had not gotten involved in."
  "How do you work best with people?"
  "What's most important to you when you work with people?"

Job-Related Criterion: Verbal Skills
What to Look for in Interview
  Candidate's comments to listen for:
    ▪ Gives straightforward, easy-to-understand answers.
    ▪ Uses words correctly and is grammatical.
    ▪ Clearly explains ideas, situations, and events.
    ▪ Phrases complex statements in easy-to-follow manner.
    ▪ Mumbles
    ▪ Speaks loudly enough to hear.
  Nonverbal actions to watch for:
    ▪ Shows difficulty finding right words to use.
    ▪ Has hard time getting words out of mouth.
Sample Questions to Ask
    There are no specific questions to ask to evaluate a person's verbal skills. Just listen throughout the interview to how candidates express themselves.

Job-Related Criterion: Persuasiveness
What to Look for in Interview
  Candidate's comments to listen for:
    ▪ Makes comments that sway interviewer.

- Displays mannerisms that interviewer finds convincing.
- Gives answers that satisfy interviewer that candidate is right on some potentially controversial topic.
- "Sells" interviewer on his qualifications for job.

Nonverbal actions to watch for:
- Looks interviewer in the eye.
- Seems to have figured out how to appeal to each interviewer, even though interviewers exhibit a variety of interpersonal styles.

Sample Questions to Ask
"Describe to me a situation in which you got people to change from the way they were doing something to the way you had suggested. How did you accomplish this?"
"Tell me about an unpopular idea you had that you were able to sell to people at work."
"Think of a time when you needed to get your boss to change the way he or she handled something. What was the situation, and how did you handle it?"
"Describe a time when you failed to sell your proposal or viewpoint to other people. What did you do wrong?"
"Tell me about two times when people disagreed with you. What did you do in each situation?"

Job-Related Criterion: Tact
What to Look for in Interview
Candidate's comments to listen for:
- Disagrees tactfully.
- Shows respect for others' viewpoints.
- Mentions being bothered by other people's bad or rude manners.
- Takes the "politics" of a situation into account before taking action.

Nonverbal actions to watch for:
- Is polite and mannerly.
- Shows consideration.
- Expresses self tactfully.
- Treats everyone with respect before, during, and after interviews.
- Is pleasant with receptionist or secretary.
- Does not act bothered if interview schedule does not go according to plan.

(continues)

Exhibit 2-6 *(continued)*

Sample Questions to Ask

"Tell me about a situation in which your boss was upset with the way you did something. How did you handle your boss?"

"How did you handle an unfounded complaint about something you did?"

"Describe a situation in which you were in a meeting with people who were above you in rank and you disagreed with an important comment made by one of those people. How did you express your disagreement?"

"What's your method of giving someone bad news?"

"Think of a time when you had to work with a very sensitive or highly emotional person. What did you do to help you get along with that individual?"

Job-Related Criterion: Candidness

What to Look for in Interview

Candidate's comments to listen for:

- Openly acknowledges problems or mistakes.
- Answers questions about his/her weaknesses.
- Readily admits difficulties.
- Does not try to hide potentially negative information.

Nonverbal actions to watch for:

- Does not hesitate before admitting problems.
- Does not flinch or look uncomfortable while discussing errors he/she made.

Sample Questions to Ask

"What's the biggest mistake you made on that job?"

"When did you really put your foot in your mouth?"

"Describe a project you fouled up."

"Tell me about the stickiest situation you faced in that job."

"What did you dislike about that job/boss/co-worker?"

"What's the biggest mistake you have made in your entire career?"

Personality Traits

Job-Related Criterion: Persistence

What to Look for in Interview

Candidate's comments to listen for:

- Completes long-term projects.
- Is tenacious despite encountering roadblocks.
- Resolves to finish whatever he or she starts.

Nonverbal actions to watch for:
- Shows pride in completing long-term or difficult projects.
- Looks for work experience that rewards the persistence needed to earn a degree or to attain certain positions.

Sample Questions to Ask
"Describe the project you are proudest of having completed."
"Tell me about some long-term projects you did."
"What's been the most difficult project for you to see through to completion?"
"How do you plan to accomplish long-range assignments?"
"What hurdles did you overcome to get as far as you've gotten in your career?"
"How do you deal with other people's procrastination?"
"Your résumé indicates that you did not complete your [degree or other goal]. What happened?"

Job-Related Criterion: Creativity
What to Look for in Interview
Candidate's comments to listen for:
- Generates imaginative solutions.
- Reports tackling projects in innovative ways.
- Mentions completing tasks without always following the procedures or rules laid out.
- Enjoys creative endeavors.
- Plays with ideas and alternatives.

Nonverbal actions to watch for:
- Smiles confidently when describing innovative methods.
- Spends more time reporting on imaginative problem solving than on uncreative problem solving.

Sample Questions to Ask
"What are the two projects you are proudest of having completed?"
"Tell me about your most difficult assignment. How did you go about it?"
"How do you lay out your plans to achieve your goals?"
"What were the tasks in your last job in which you could try out new ideas or ways of doing things?"
"Describe a problem for which your first solution did not work, so that you were forced to try other solutions."
"How do you help other people to solve their work problems?"

(continues)

Exhibit 2-6   *(continued)*

Job-Related Criterion: Follows Rules and Procedures
What to Look for in Interview
  Candidate's comments to listen for:
    ▪ Likes working "by the book."
    ▪ Shows concern for established ways of carrying out tasks.
    ▪ Refers to policy or procedure manuals.
    ▪ Mentions using traditionally accepted methods.
  Nonverbal actions to watch for:
    ▪ Has neater appearance than is typical.
    ▪ Looks uncomfortable when referring to trying new methods.
Sample Questions to Ask
  "How do you decide how to tackle a new assignment?"
  "When you are given another employee's tasks to do, how do you
    determine how to handle them?"
  "Describe a big project you worked on. How did you figure out
    what to do?"
  "What do you take into account when you have to plan and com-
    plete an objective?"

Job-Related Criterion: Handles Obstacles Well
What to Look for in Interview
  Candidate's comments to listen for:
    ▪ Mentions bouncing back from defeats or downfalls.
    ▪ Is emotionally objective when discussing hurdles.
    ▪ Views problems as opportunities in disguise.
    ▪ Develops skills through overcoming roadblocks.
  Nonverbal actions to watch for:
    ▪ Relishes chance to show resilience.
    ▪ Looks confident about tackling obstacles.
Sample Questions to Ask
  "What were the most difficult problems you encountered in that
    job? What did you do about them?"
  "What was your reaction to that roadblock?"
  "How would you advise someone who is having trouble in finish-
    ing an assignment?"

Job-Related Criterion: Optimism
What to Look for in Interview
  Candidate's comments to listen for:
    ▪ Focuses on solutions rather than problems.
    ▪ Happily grapples with solutions to any problems.
    ▪ Has a can-do attitude.

- Enjoys overcoming obstacles.
- Does not mention feeling burned out or overly stressed.

Nonverbal actions to watch for:

- Expresses enthusiasm and exuberance.
- Appears confident.
- Shows pride in describing accomplishments.

Sample Questions to Ask

"Tell me about the worst situation you ever got into in any job."

"What are some other problems you encountered in that job?"

"What types of work attitudes do you like to see in other people?"

"What attitudes have helped you to achieve as much as you have in your career?"

Job-Related Criterion: High Energy

What to Look for in Interview

Candidate's comments to listen for:

- Does not indicate feeling worn out even after putting in long hours at work.
- Exerts effort with vigor and great stamina.
- Likes physically moving, not just sitting in one place.

Nonverbal actions to watch for:

- Maintains high energy level throughout interview.
- Exudes zest and vitality.

Sample Questions to Ask

"What sort of hours per week do you give to your job?"

"How many assignments do you like to work on at one time?"

"What do you do when you have lots of tasks to complete and only a very limited number of days in which to do them? Give me some examples of how you've handled such situations."

"Describe your most effective time-management techniques."

Job-Related Criterion: Focusing on Feelings or *Focusing on Facts*

What to Look for in Interview

Candidate's comments to listen for:

- Feeling-Focused: Mentions emotions and personal issues.
- Fact-Focused: Mentions basics and actual details of jobs.

Nonverbal actions to watch for:

- Shows more interest in feelings/facts when responding to questions.

Sample Questions to Ask

"What do you tell yourself you must do the first time you have to deal with a new prospect or customer? with a co-worker? with an executive?"

(continues)

Exhibit 2-6   *(continued)*

"When you first approach someone you must talk with, what do you tend to do?"

"How do you weigh the relative importance of handling feelings versus handling facts in your relationships at work? Give some examples of how you do this."

"What factors have contributed most to your success in dealing with people in your various jobs?"

Job-Related Criterion: Poise Under Pressure

What to Look for in Interview

Candidate's comments to listen for:

- Describes thriving under pressure or stress.
- Mentions feeling burned out or overloaded.
- Indicates getting upset or out of emotional control.
- Focuses on anxiety or nervousness.

Nonverbal actions to watch for:

- Seems to enjoy interview.
- Twitches, trembles, or blinks excessively while talking.
- Has sweaty palms when shaking hands.

Sample Questions to Ask

"Tell me about some really high-pressure situations you've experienced on that job."

"What most drives you up the wall at work?"

"How do you handle the frustration you feel with your co-workers? your customers? your boss?"

"What most discourages or frustrates you on your job?"

"What do you do to vent your work-related stress?"

Job-Related Criterion: Being a Self-Starter

What to Look for in Interview

Candidate's comments to listen for:

- Tackles tasks and projects without being prompted.
- Sets goals and goes on to achieve them.
- Expresses no need to be told what to do by others.
- Bristles at being told when to start assignments.

Nonverbal actions to watch for:

- Exudes pride when talking about showing initiative.

Sample Questions to Ask

"How did you get started on two recent assignments you handled?"

"What's your approach, in general, to kicking off a new project?"

"To what extent does your boss watch over what you do?"

"In general, how does work get assigned to you? What's your role
in this process?"

"What have you done to anticipate business trends that proved useful to you on your job? Give me examples."

"What reading do you do related to your work? [Listen to answer.]
Summarize one of those articles/books you just mentioned."

Motivations
Job-Related Criterion: Being Achievement-Oriented
What to Look for in Interview
> Candidate's comments to listen for:
> > ▪ Continually mentions results achieved.
> > ▪ Focuses more on outcomes than on the process used to reach
> > outcomes.
> > ▪ Is enthusiastic about getting things done.
> > ▪ Lets interviewer know about accomplishments.
> Nonverbal actions to watch for:
> > ▪ Gets to the point readily.

Sample Questions to Ask
> "What are some of the objectives you tackled on your job?"
> "What matters most to you in your work?"
> "What do you constantly keep in mind while you work on
> projects?"
> "What would make you suitable for this job?"

Job-Related Criterion: Desire for High Earnings
What to Look for in Interview
> Candidate's comments to listen for:
> > ▪ Mentions financial achievements.
> > ▪ Is enthusiastic about earning incentive pay.
> > ▪ Links work results to compensation.
> > ▪ Desires to earn money for a specific purchase, e.g., a home,
> > nicer car, clothes, furniture.
> Nonverbal actions to watch for:
> > ▪ Wears expensive clothing.
> > ▪ Drives an expensive car.

Sample Questions to Ask
> "All in all, when you come to work each day, what's the one ingredi-
> ent of your job that makes you feel most enthusiastic?"
> "Describe the ideal compensation plan for you."

(continues)

Exhibit 2-6   *(continued)*

"How would you like your pay to be determined?"
"What most inspires you to do a good job?"
"Tell me what you would like to get out of this job, if you get it."

Job-Related Criterion: Desire to Help People
What to Look for in Interview
    Candidate's comments to listen for:
        ▪ Enjoys assisting and serving people.
        ▪ Goes out of his or her way to aid others.
    Nonverbal actions to watch for:
        ▪ Offers to help interviewer, e.g., by getting coffee.
        ▪ Shows extra interest when talking about helping people.
Sample Questions to Ask
    "All in all, when you come to work each day, what's the one ingredi-
        ent of your job that gives you the greatest satisfaction?"
    "What most inspires you to do a good job?"
    "What would you like to get out of this job, if you are hired?"
    "Describe your ideal job."
    "If you could spend more time doing any particular activities that
        form part of your job, what would they be?"

Job-Related Criterion: Desire to Do Creative Work
What to Look for in Interview
    Candidate's comments to listen for:
        ▪ Loves doing innovative work.
        ▪ Goes out of his or her way to find imaginative solutions to
            problems.
    Nonverbal actions to watch for:
        ▪ Wears nontraditional clothing.
Sample Questions to Ask
    "All in all, when you come to work each day, what's the one ingredi-
        ent of your job that makes you feel most enthusiastic?"
    "What most inspires you to do a good job?"
    "What would you like to get out of this job, if you are offered it?"
    "Describe your ideal job."
    "If you could spend more time on particular aspects of your work,
        what would they be?"

Job-Related Criterion: Desire for Power
What to Look for in Interview
    Candidate's comments to listen for:
        ▪ Likes to exercise authority.
        ▪ Goes out of his or her way to control work situations.

Nonverbal actions to watch for:
- Acts like a take-charge person in interview.
- Tries to control flow of interview.

Sample Questions to Ask
"All in all, when you come to work each day, what's the one ingredient of your job that makes you feel most enthusiastic?"
"What most inspires you to do a good job?"
"What would you like to get out of this job, if you get it?"
"Describe your ideal job."
"If you could spend more time doing particular aspects of your work, what would they be?"

Job-Related Criterion: Desire to Increase Knowledge
What to Look for in Interview
Candidate's comments to listen for:
- Loves doing "research" and learning from job.
- Goes out of his or her way to uncover data or other information.
- Asks interviewer for information on a variety of work-related matters, e.g., company facts and figures, history of job.

Nonverbal actions to watch for:
- Shows alertness to new information.

Sample Questions to Ask
"All in all, when you come to work each day, what's the one ingredient of your job that makes you feel most enthusiastic?"
"What most inspires you to do a good job?"
"What would you like to get out of this job, if you are offered it?"
"Describe your ideal job."
"If you could spend more time on particular features of your work, what would they be?"

Management and Leadership
Job-Related Criterion: Planning Skills
What to Look for in Interview
Candidate's comments to listen for:
- Mentions developing long-term plans covering one or more years.
- Explains achievements in terms of executing plans.
- Sets priorities, timetables, and deadlines.

(continues)

Exhibit 2-6   *(continued)*

Nonverbal actions to watch for:
  - Shows enthusiasm when talking about planning.
Sample Questions to Ask
  "How do you schedule your work?"
  "How did you go about accomplishing some of your long-term goals?"
  "When you show up at work in the morning, how do you know what to do each day?"
  "Describe how you managed change in your organization."
  "What targets must your department accomplish, and how do you make sure those targets are reached?"

Job-Related Criterion: Organizing Skills
What to Look for in Interview
  Candidate's comments to listen for:
    - Mentions getting work done in logical fashion.
    - Pays special attention to organizing work flow.
    - Makes sure each employee knows how his/her work fits into department's overall strategy.
  Nonverbal actions to watch for:
    - Shows delight at the mention of using checklists.
Sample Questions to Ask
  "What targets are your department responsible for accomplishing, and how do you make sure those targets are reached?"
  "How do you decide what each employee in your department needs to do?"

Job-Related Criterion: Delegating and Controlling Skills
What to Look for in Interview
  Candidate's comments to listen for:
    - Assigns tasks to subordinates.
    - Follows up on work delegated.
    - Specifies quantity and quality of work expected from employees.
    - Personally inspects work of others to ensure that it is on target.
  Nonverbal actions to watch for:
    N/A
Sample Questions to Ask
  "What steps do you take to make sure your department produces quality work?"

"What is your system for ensuring that work gets done correctly and on time?"

"What methods do you use when you delegate work? Give examples."

"How do you make sure that your subordinates provide good service to other departments or customers?"

"Describe some of your employees who were very difficult to manage and how you handled them."

Job-Related Criterion: Skills in Motivating Others
What to Look for in Interview
Candidate's comments to listen for:
- Mentions improving employees' morale.
- Talks about how he or she influences employees to increase productivity.
- Describes management techniques his or her employees liked.

Nonverbal actions to watch for:
N/A

Sample Questions to Ask
"How have you influenced your employees to increase their productivity? Give some examples of what you did."

"No two employees are exactly alike. How do you take this into account when you manage them?"

"What sort of turnover or absenteeism problems have you had to deal with?"

"Tell me about a particularly difficult employee you were able to turn around and help to become a good, solid worker."

COGNITIVE JOB-RELATED CRITERIA

Mental Abilities

Note: Mental abilities are evaluated mainly on the basis of tests, since such abilities are generally hard to pinpoint in a job interview. Some of the mental abilities assessed by tests include the following:
- Reasoning/problem-solving ability
- Vocabulary ability
- Arithmetic/computations ability
- Grammar, spelling, and correct word usage
- Ability to handle details with speed and accuracy

(continues)

Exhibit 2-6   *(continued)*

Technical Job Knowledge and Skills

Job-Related Criterion: Knowledge of _____
(fill in)

What to Look for in Interview
 Candidate's comments to listen for:
  ▪ Indicates possession of knowledge relevant to doing the job.
  ▪ Is conversant with job-related knowledge or information.
 Nonverbal actions to watch for:
  ▪ Notice if applicant speaks haltingly or comfortably when
   questioned about job-related knowledge or information.
Sample Questions to Ask
 "Describe to me how _____ works."
 "What is the research on how to do _____?"
 "Tell me about your experiences using _____."

Job-Related Criterion: Skill in Doing _____
(fill in)

What to Look for in Interview
 Candidate's comments to listen for:
  ▪ Mentions using specific skills on the job.
  ▪ Describes applying the skills.
 Nonverbal actions to watch for:
  N/A
Sample Questions to Ask
 "What sort of training did you have to develop and use
  your _____ skills?"
 "How have you used your _____ skills on the job?"
 "What improvements have you made in using your _____
  skills at work?"

Thinking Techniques

Job-Related Criterion: Organized Thinking
What to Look for in Interview
 Candidate's comments to listen for:
  ▪ Orders phrasing in answering questions.
  ▪ Is logical.
  ▪ Uses or makes lists while talking to refer to the solution to
   some problem in three steps.
 Nonverbal actions to watch for:
  N/A

Sample Questions to Ask
> "Tell me about your work history."
> "What jobs have you held?"
> "How did you carry out that project?"
> "How might you have handled that project differently?"
> "What are the biggest problems facing your employer?"

Job-Related Criterion: Detail-Focused Thinking
What to Look for in Interview
> Candidate's comments to listen for:
> - Mentions many details.
> - Tells you how to conduct a project, not just what the results of it are.
> - Digs for reasons automatically without being prompted to do so.
>
> Nonverbal actions to wach for:
> N/A

Sample Questions to Ask
> "Tell me about a big assignment you handled recently. How did you tackle it?"
> "When you had problems, how did you recognize them before they had a chance to get bigger?"
> "What's a major problem you took care of? What did you do to solve it?"
> "How would you compare and contrast _____ and _____?"

Job-Related Criterion: Whole-Picture Thinking
What to Look for in Interview
> Candidate's comments to listen for:
> - Does not get bogged down in details at the expense of the big picture.
> - Emphasizes the purpose and results of a project rather than the way it was executed.
> - Describes how his or her job contributes to the company's overall success.
> - Understands the impact of economic, political, and industry factors on his or her employer.
>
> Nonverbal actions to watch for:
> N/A

Sample Questions to Ask
> "How does your job fit with your company's overall goals?"

(continues)

Exhibit 2-6   *(continued)*

"How do national or global economic factors affect your employer?"

"What's going on in your employer's industry that directly affects your company?"

Job-Related Criterion: Objectivity in Decision Making
What to Look for in Interview
Candidate's comments to listen for:
- Relies on research indicating probable results more than on intuition.
- Does not let emotions get in way of judgment.

Nonverbal actions to watch for:
N/A
Sample Questions to Ask
"Describe a big decision you made in that job. How did you arrive at that decision?"

"Describe a sticky situation you faced with an employee and how you resolved it?"

"Tell me about a decision you made that did not work out well. How did you reach that decision?"

"When you must make a choice between two ways of doing something, how do you make your decision? Give an example."

Job-Related Criterion: Intuitive Decision Making
What to Look for in Interview
Candidate's comments to listen for:
- Uses gut feelings in making decisions in conjunction with research indicating probable results.
- Lets emotions sway judgment.

Nonverbal actions to watch for:
N/A
Sample Questions to Ask
"Describe an important decision you made on the job. How did you arrive at that decision?"

"What was a sticky situation you faced with an employee, and how did you resolve it?"

"Tell me about a decision you made that did not work out well. How did you make that decision?"

"When you must decide between two alternative ways of doing something, how do you go about making your choice? Give an example."

Exhibit 2-2. But it goes beyond the Job Analysis Checklist to lay before you what you should be looking for in the interview and the kind of questions you should ask.

Most important when asking questions, you must always keep in mind the position's six to nine job-related criteria. Then, you must be on the lookout for *patterns* in the candidate's comments or ways of behaving that give insight into his or her talent with respect to each criterion.

For example, on the criterion of friendliness, you might find a pattern if the applicant repeatedly spoke of these things:

- Enjoying socializing
- Looking forward to being around people
- Doing things with friends

Or you might look to the first impressions you have gained of the candidate's personality—his smiles or other outgoing behavior—for clues as to his friendliness.

The Interview Guide Form: A Customized Way to Take Highly Useful Interview Notes

After you've used Exhibit 2-2 to create a list of the six to nine most crucial job-related criteria for a particular job, and Exhibit 2-6 to pinpoint what to look for and ask in the interview it is time to create a simple, customized Interview Guide Form for each position. The Interview Guide Form provides a convenient way for you to remember what job-related criteria to look for and to take readily useful notes during the interview.

One Interview Guide Form is designed for *each* job for which managers will interview applicants. An original or master copy of the Interview Guide Form for each position can be stored in a computer or a file folder. Then, whenever you or other managers interview candidates for a job, each interviewer must receive a copy of the Interview Guide Form for that specific position. By following this procedure, all interviewers:

- Know what job-related criteria to focus on while interviewing candidates for a certain position.
- Take notes on the same job-related criteria being used.
- Participate in post-interview meetings and discussions of each applicant using the same criteria, same definitions, and same rating system.

Each Interview Guide Form contains the following ten ingredients:

1. Job title for which the Interview Guide Form has been customized
2. Candidate's name
3. Date of interview
4. Interviewer's name
5. Job-related criteria (see Exhibit 2-2)
6. What to look for to evaluate an applicant on each criterion
7. Space for taking notes
8. Rating of candidate on each job-related criterion using arrow ratings

↑	=positive rating, in effect, a 12 o'clock or 1 o'clock arrow
→	=average or neutral rating, in effect, a 2 o'clock, 3 o'clock, or 4 o'clock arrow
↓	=negative rating, in effect, a 5 o'clock or 6 o'clock arrow

9. Space for additional observations or notes (optional)
10. Overall rating of the candidate using the arrow technique

Exhibit 2-7 is an example of an Interview Guide Form for a salesperson's job. Sample Interview Guide Forms for the positions of secretary and manager appear in Appendix A and Appendix B, respectively. The job-related criteria shown in these three Interview Guide Forms previously appeared in Exhibits 2-3, 2-4, and 2-5.

Exhibit 2-7. Example of an Interview Guide Form for sales candidates.

<hr>

INTERVIEW GUIDE FORM
for CANDIDATE FOR *SALESPERSON*

CANDIDATE'S NAME: _____

INTERVIEWER'S NAME: _____

DATE OF INTERVIEW: _____

Instructions

As you interview a candidate, focus on evaluating the person on the job-related criteria shown on this interview guide form. Be sure to take notes during the interview in the space provided.

After the interview, rate the candidate by circling the appropriate arrow to:

- Rate candidate on each job-related criterion.
- Give candidate overall rating at end of this form.

NOTE: ↑ = Positive rating
        → = Average rating
        ↓ = Negative rating

Job-Related Criterion	*Ratings and Notes*
Assertiveness	Notes:
_____ Takes charge of projects or tasks.	
_____ Does not back off.	
_____ Expresses opinions firmly.	
_____ Lets interviewer know his/her viewpoints.	
	Rating: ↓ → ↑
Prefers Working Solo	Notes:
_____ Enjoys working alone.	
_____ Seldom mentions working with others.	
_____ Gives minimal praise to group work efforts.	

(continues)

Exhibit 2-7   *(continued)*

_____ Describes being most productive when
       alone.

Rating: ↓ → ↑

Persuasiveness   Notes:
_____ Sways others' opinions and actions.
_____ Sells interviewer on himself/herself.
_____ Describes influencing others of diverse in-
       terpersonal styles.

Rating: ↓ → ↑

Handles Obstacles Well   Notes:
_____ Bounces back, shows resilience.
_____ Is emotionally objective.
_____ Views problems as opportunities in dis-
       guise.
_____ Gives examples of overcoming road-
       blocks.

Rating: ↓ → ↑

Optimism   Notes:
_____ Focuses on solutions, not problems.
_____ Focuses on opportunities, not drawbacks.
_____ Has "Can-Do" attitude.
_____ Does not mention burn-out or high
       stress.

Rating: ↓ → ↑

High Energy   Notes:
_____ Is tireless.
_____ Shows great stamina.
_____ Likes being very busy.
_____ Remains highly energetic throughout in-
       terview.

Rating: ↓ → ↑

Being a Self-Starter   Notes:
_____ Gives examples of showing initiative.
_____ Has history of taking responsibility and
       being a self-starter.
_____ Mentions doing tasks without being
       prodded.
_____ Dislikes being told what to do.

Rating: ↓ → ↑

Desire for High Earnings   Notes:
_____ Often mentions earning $.
_____ Discusses financial achievements and/or
      goals.
_____ Is enthusiastic about earning incentive
      pay.
_____ Craves pay linked to results.

Rating: ↓   →   ↑

OVERALL RATING OF THIS CANDIDATE: ↓   →   ↑

3

Interviews for Forecasting a Candidate's Success on the Job

Part II: How to Conduct Interviews and Evaluate Job Candidates

After doing a job analysis and creating an Interview Guide Form, as explained in Chapter 2, your next actions include:

1. Interviewing candidates
2. Meeting with others who interviewed the same candidates
3. Filling in the Candidate Rating Sheet on each candidate*

Six Essentials of All Effective Interviews

Interviewers who keep certain basics in mind can do well when interviewing job candidates. The six essentials of all effective interviews, given in brief in Exhibit 3-1, are as follows:

1. *Do a quick, yet exacting, job analysis.* This specifies the job-related criteria required of a candidate who is capable of

---

*This chapter also explains legal guidelines to keep in mind while interviewing applicants.

Exhibit 3-1.   Essentials of face-to-face interviewing.

1. Do job analysis using Job Analysis Checklist [see Exhibit 2-2].
2. Take notes during each interview on the customized Interview Guide Form you created for the specific job.
3. Always remember this principle: *Past behavior is the best predictor of future behavior.*
4. From your observation of the candidate's nonverbal behavior, ask yourself this question: Do the words go with the music?
5. Keep in mind that the behavior you see in the interview is likely to be the best behavior you will ever see from the candidate if you hire him/her.
6. Ask other people who saw the candidate how he/she acted with them.

succeeding in a particular job. Such job analyses can be accomplished easily with the help of the Job Analysis Checklist shown in Exhibit 2-2.

2. Take notes during the interview. It is amazing how often managers fail to take notes during interviews. Or if they take them, their comments turn out to be useless. Why does this happen? Some interviewers simply do not know what to write. Yet this problem vanishes when a customized Interview Guide Form is used.

Other interviewers figure that they can take notes after the interview. Lots of luck!! Often after an interview, a busy manager forgets key points or gets distracted by a rash of conversations, meetings, or phone calls. By the next day, that manager won't have a clue as to what to write about an applicant.

Both excuses for not taking notes must be avoided. It is necessary to take notes so that a useful record of the interview will be available for a later discussion and rating of each candidate.

3. Remember the principle that past behavior is the best predictor of future behavior. How can you spot behavior patterns relevant to the job? Continually:

- Ask for specific *examples* of projects, tasks, or assignments the candidate has handled.
- Probe for *details* on how the candidate actually went about this work.

- Look for *patterns* in how the candidate accomplished these tasks.

For instance, imagine that you want to hire someone for a job in which creative problem solving is crucial. When you ask Candidate A to describe projects she did, she repeatedly describes carrying out projects by conscientiously following step-by-step procedures laid out by someone else. In contrast, Candidate B continually talks about tackling projects by conjuring up new methods or variations of previously used procedures. Question: Given their answers, which candidate would be more likely to use creative problem solving on the job? Of course, Candidate B emerges as much more likely than Candidate A to use creative problem solving. After all, Candidate B's interview responses reveal a pattern of giving specific, detailed examples of having used creative problem solving, whereas Candidate A's responses reveal the opposite.

4. *Observe the candidate's nonverbal behavior.* Another way of putting this is, ask yourself: Do the words go with the music? I once interviewed a management applicant who repeatedly mentioned how much he "loved dealing with people," and that this was partly why he sought the management position; yet he avoided most eye contact; often put his hands over his mouth while talking; and periodically spoke so softly that he was hard to hear. In this case, the words sounded on target for this particular management job, which required lots of personal interaction. However, his "music" sang a different song. This music included (1) avoiding eye contact, (2) putting his hands over his mouth while talking, and (3) sometimes becoming difficult to hear. Such "music" betrays the candidate's game by showing that his words expressing how much he enjoyed contact with people are a sham. An interviewer who listened only to the words without taking the "music," or nonverbal behavior, into account would miss such make-or-break data about the candidate.

5. *Ask other people who saw the candidate how that person behaved.* During one of the first interviews I ever conducted, I felt awed by how sharp-witted and charming the job applicant seemed. After I showed him out the door following the inter-

view, I exclaimed, "Wow, what a candidate!" (meaning what a great candidate) to which the receptionist replied, "Yeah, what a jerk!" The receptionist then revealed that while waiting for me to interview him, the applicant had *complained* about the magazines in the waiting room, the lighting level in that area, the coffee the receptionist gave him, and the attire of certain employees. The candidate had put on a magnificent show during the interview, and at that early point in my career I was not astute enough to detect the negative, complaining, grumbling behavior the receptionist immediately noticed.

6. *Keep in mind that the behavior you see during the interview is likely to be the best behavior you'll ever see from that person.* Why is this true? Because candidates usually are on their best behavior during the applicant screening process. After they are hired and have been on the job for a while, people get used to their boss and co-workers and resume habitual ways of acting.

For instance, let's say that you want to hire a mannerly person for a particular job. If Candidate A acts in a very mannerly fashion during the interview, then if you hire Candidate A you can expect her to act very mannerly—or worse—on the job. By the same token, if Candidate B acts in an unmannerly fashion during the interview, then you can expect her to act that unmannerly—or even worse—if hired. People tend to act the same or worse after they are hired. They seldom behave better on the job.

The Two Types of Interview Questions

There are only two types of questions in the world: closed-ended questions and open-ended questions[1]:

1. *Closed-ended questions.* These ask the candidate to:
   - Answer yes or no, or pick X or Y.
   - Think very little.
   - Talk very little.
2. Open-ended questions. These result in the candidate:
   - Not being able to answer with a quick yes or no, or X or Y.

- Thinking before answering.
- Talking more, especially about
  —Thoughts
  —Needs
  —Feelings
  —Opinions
  —Experiences
  —Interests
  —Goals

As candidates answer open-ended questions, they invariably reveal the presence or absence or level of these crucial job-related factors:

- Interpersonal skills
- Communications skills
- Personality traits
- Motivations
- Intelligence
- Organizational skills and thinking
- Technical knowledge, skills, and abilities

Examples of closed-ended questions and of their open-ended counterparts appear in Exhibit 3-2.

The first closed-ended question shown in Exhibit 3-2, "Did you like your last job?" requires only a short yes or no answer. It does not call for the candidate to think much or to reveal her thoughts, needs, feelings, and opinions.

By contrast, the corresponding open-ended inquiry, "Tell me about your last job," calls for the applicant to think before answering, to organize her thoughts, and to discuss the work experience in such a way that her interests, goals, needs, and feelings are revealed.

As the applicant answers this open-ended item, she conceivably could choose from among hundreds of possible answers. She might, for example, address the following topics:

- How she liked or disliked her last job
- The duties assigned her

Exhibit 3-2. Closed-ended versus open-ended questions.

Closed-Ended Question	Open-Ended Question
"Did you like your last job?"	"Tell me about your last job."
"Was your boss helpful to you?"	"What was your boss like?"
"Did you use creative problem solving in that job?"	"Describe specific problems you dealt with and how you handled them."
"Is this enjoyable work for you?"	"How do you feel about this sort of work?"

- Work conditions in her company
- Projects undertaken or participated in
- Her co-workers
- Training received on the job

Whatever she says helps the interviewer to form an opinion by revealing the applicant's:

- Interpersonal skills
- Communications skills
- Personality traits
- Motivations
- Intelligence level
- Style of thinking (organized or disorganized)
- Technical knowledge, skills, and abilities

The applicant's answers and ways of answering of course are related, either positively or negatively, to the criteria for the job, and open-ended questions do much to clarify the connections, or lack of connections, for the interviewer.

Each of the other three closed-ended and open-ended questions in Exhibit 3-2 also illustrate the same point: Open-ended probes can reveal a great deal more about an applicant than closed-ended questions do. This underscores the need for interviewers to rely primarily on open-ended questions. In fact, closed-ended questions prove useful mainly when the interviewer needs to have specific information, direct answers to such questions as "Can you use ABC equipment?" or "Did you ever use XYZ software?" or "Is it possible for you to work our normal business hours plus some overtime?"

Based on my experience training thousands of managers, it is apparent to me that prior to training, most interviewers (1) do not know what questions to ask, and (2) rely overwhelmingly on closed-ended questions.

Amazingly, many of the closed-ended questions that the average interviewer asks virtually give away the correct answer. For instance, a typical interviewer may ask the closed-ended question, "Did you use creative problem solving in that job?" Any candidate with an IQ of room temperature or higher instantly realizes the exact answer the interviewer wants to hear, namely, "Yes, I used creative problem solving." By asking such closed-ended questions, many interviewers unknowingly enable candidates to come across as vastly more capable than they really are. This, in turn, contributes to the typically poor ability of most interviewers to accurately predict on-the-job behavior.

A better way to discover the same information about a candidate's creative problem-solving ability would be to use an open-ended probe, such as "Describe some problems you dealt with and how you handled them." Then, listening for repeated patterns in what the candidate says, you can detect if the candidate used creative problem-solving techniques or noncreative problem-solving methods. The advantage of the open-ended inquiry is that it never reveals to the candidate that the interviewer wants to hire someone who is definitely experienced in creative problem solving.

Fortunately, it is relatively easy to word open-ended questions. To get the hang of it, just use the words or phrases shown in Exhibit 3-3.

The Dangers of Talking Too Much

How much talking should an interviewer do? A competent interviewer should talk only 10 to 20 percent of the interview time. This allows the candidate to talk for 80 to 90 percent of the time. Why this one-sided allotment? The reason is that the purpose of a job interview is for the interviewer to find out about the

Exhibit 3-3. Words commonly starting closed-ended and open-ended questions.

Words Commonly Starting Closed-Ended Questions	*Words Commonly Starting Open-Ended Questions*
"Do . . . ?"	"What . . . ?"
"Is . . . ?"	"How . . . ?"
"Was . . . ?"	"Tell me about . . . ."
	"Describe . . . ."

candidate, *not* for the candidate to hear the interviewer blab. The more the applicant talks, the more the interviewer can discover about the person's job-related knowledge, skills, and abilities.

In fact, one way for a candidate to detect that the interviewer does not know what he is doing is for the interviewer to do most of the talking. Doing so usually indicates that the interviewer is unenlightened about how to interview and unskilled in how to predict from the interview whether or not the applicant really can do the job.

However, because many interviewers do not know how to conduct an interview, it seems important here to point out what an overly talkative interviewer tends to do. Specifically, such a chatterbox often inadvertently:

- *Tells the applicant too many details about what specific job skills are needed.* Armed with this overly precise information, any moderately bright candidate can tell the interviewer that she just happens to be gloriously adept at exactly those very specific skills needed to succeed in the job.
- *Fails to uncover the applicant's actual job-related knowledge, skills, and abilities.*
- *Uses mainly closed-ended questions.* In doing so, the interviewer:
  —Seldom finds out whether the candidate meets the job-related criteria.
  —Implies that the candidate is restricted to yes or no or X or Y answers.

—Spends so much time thinking of the next closed-ended question that he does not have time to listen carefully to the candidate's brief response.
- *Calms his own anxiety by chattering at the expense of eliciting the most important information from the applicant.*

The Best Physical Arrangements for an Interview

Three main physical arrangements ought to be made before each interview.

1. *Arrange to hold the interview in a private room.* The room should have a door that can be closed during the interview to ensure privacy. It is distracting to hold an interview in an open area where anyone can walk by or eavesdrop on what the two of you are saying. Also, holding the interview in a nonprivate area could give the impression that the company is unconcerned about privacy rights or confidentiality.

2. *Always avoid interruptions during the interview.* In other words, do *not* make phone calls or answer the phone, and do *not* allow anyone to come into the interview room. Basically, allow an interruption only if the building is burning down! All other intrusions disrupt the interview and show disrespect for the applicant.

3. *Place chairs in an optimal seating arrangement.* In general, it gives a somewhat authoritarian or unfriendly impression to have the interviewer sitting behind a desk while the candidate sits in front of the desk. A more cordial seating arrangement is one in which the interviewer's and candidate's chairs are either directly facing each other or at a 45-degree angle to one another, with no desk between the interviewer and the candidate.

Four Topics to Cover in a Great Interview

What are the most important subjects an interviewer should ask about during an interview? The four that are the most basic, cover the greatest amount of territory, and are most likely to generate crucial information about the candidate are the following:

1. Work history or experiences
2. Education and training
3. Career goals or aspirations
4. Anything else the candidate wants to add or ask

Answers to an array of questions on these four subjects yield information on and insights into the candidate in terms of the six to nine job-related criteria that appear on the Interview Guide Form. The interviewer takes notes as this information unfolds.

The way to start the interview, after an initial couple of minutes devoted to helping the candidate feel comfortable, is to state:

> We'll delve into four main subjects in this interview: First is your work history or experiences, second is your education and training, third is your career goals or aspirations, and fourth is anything else you want to add or any questions you want to ask.

Use mainly open-ended questions and very few closed-ended questions. This works best, as we've seen, because open-ended questions make the candidate both think harder and reveal more information that is relevant to the crucial job-related criteria.

For instance, start interviewing on the first subject by stating to the candidate, "Tell me about your work history or experiences." After completing that topic, launch into the second topic with another open-ended inquiry, "Tell me about your education and training."

Use the same open-ended approach to initiate the other two interview subjects. For the third subject, start by asking, "What are your career goals or aspirations?" Later in the interview, lead into the fourth subject by asking, "What questions, if any, would you like to ask me? Or would you like to add to or clarify anything we've already talked about?"

As the candidate talks on each subject, focus particularly on and probe into his or her choice points and change points:

- *Choice points.* These come up when the applicant mentions making a choice between alternatives or options, such as choosing a particular way to handle a project or assignment.
- *Change points.* These arise when the applicant mentions altering course, such as changing jobs, careers, or academic majors.

The pattern of how and why a candidate makes choices or changes can reveal a good deal about certain job-related criteria, such as thinking style, personality, and motivations.

When the candidate mentions a choice or change, probe how she came to make that decision. For instance, the candidate may say, "After my first job as a bookkeeper, I got a job as a salesperson." This indicates both a job choice and a career change. So, probe that. A good query could consist of either of the following:

"How did you land the sales job?"
"Why did you decide to switch from bookkeeping or financial work to sales work?"

The applicant may go on to say, "I began my job at that company as an inside salesperson. But, after six months, I started doing outside sales." As this represents still another change, investigate it. Ask, "How did you happen to make that change?" or "How did you feel about making such a change?"

You should also ask any other questions that seem appropriate from those listed in Exhibit 2-6. These questions help you to delve into the crucial job-related criteria listed on the Interview Guide Form customized for the job for which the candidate is applying. Also, jot down comments and observations on the Interview Guide Form. These notes will play a key role in helping you to rate the candidate accurately.

Determining the Length of an Interview

In general, a good interview for most jobs lasts at least one hour. For higher-level management and executive jobs, interviews should last at least two hours.

There are reasons why long interviews are helpful or even necessary. Many applicants can "talk a good talk" and come across well for an hour. However, after an hour, even a well-rehearsed candidate or world-class charmer may not be able to continue putting on such a good show. In an interview, the candidate does 80 to 90 percent of the talking, and after an hour, if he has not been totally truthful, he may start contradicting himself or tripping over what he has said earlier.

Also, the longer the interview lasts, the more patterns you can discover. For instance, in a short interview a candidate may come across as quite persistent, often a key job-related criterion. However, if the interview is extended, he may indicate some reluctance about working on long-term projects. Thus, by spending more time with the candidate, you are able to learn that while this applicant initially made the "right" comments related to persistence, he later revealed a pattern of not really liking work situations that demanded persistence.

If you had interviewed the candidate for less than one hour, you probably would have given him an up-pointing arrow, or positive evaluation, on the job-related persistence criterion. By interviewing longer, you would have learned two important things: (1) the candidate was bluffing about his real persistence level; and (2) this applicant lacked the proper qualifications for the job.

Many interviewers complain that they do not have enough time to spend an hour or more interviewing each candidate. True, managers and recruiters may be quite busy with myriad other obligations. However, in the long run it takes a lot less time to thoroughly interview each candidate than to hire the wrong person and then have to manage an average or below-average employee or, worse, terminate an employee who should not have been hired in the first place.

For instance, let's say manager Barbara Newton needs to

hire a new employee. Normally, she spends thirty minutes interviewing each applicant. She likes to interview the top three candidates for each job opening. Therefore, she typically spends an hour and a half interviewing applicants to fill each job opening. Following the suggested one-hour-or-longer interview length, she would spend only an additional hour and a half interviewing her top three candidates, or a total of three hours.

Let's say she opts for her usual thirty-minute interview instead. While she saves all of an hour and a half, a below-average candidate succeeds in making her think that he is better able to do the job than he really is. During the short, thirty-minute interview she missed some make-or-break information or insights about how the candidate would perform on the job. That is, she lowered the validity or accuracy of her interview predictions.

So, she now has a below-average employee on her hands. Isn't it likely that she will end up spending much more time than the extra hour and a half she should have spent interviewing to manage this below-average performer? Remember, this below-average employee will be less productive than desired, and if, finally, he must be terminated for poor productivity or for being a troublemaker, that process often ends up being an incredibly time-consuming, money-wasting activity. All this extra expense, time, and energy would be squandered on a below-average employee.

Yet, very possibly, all these expensive problems could have been avoided if the manager had spent only an extra hour and a half (thirty minutes extra per interview × three interviews = 1.5 hours) interviewing her top three candidates. Isn't a little more interviewing time a remarkably small price to pay for hiring the best and avoiding the rest?

A candidate for a professional position should be interviewed for no less than one to two hours. Highly paid professionals such as salespeople, engineers, and accountants do highly skilled work. Successful professionals can add a lot to the bottom line, and they are easier to train and manage. So, devoting one to two hours to each interview is really a very low-cost investment for a potentially high return.

In fact, it generally works best if each candidate for a management or executive job is interviewed for two or more hours. That may seem like a lot of time, but imagine how much money and productivity go down the drain when a below-average manager or executive is hired. Think how much better off the company would be if it had only above-average or excellent leaders.

Candidates for high-level positions are often quite skilled at answering interview questions. Sometimes they even get professional training in how to do spectacularly well in interviews. They may also have been involved in the hiring of top brass themselves, so they are apt to be familiar with the criteria the interviewer is looking for. Given these facts, it is important to do long interviews with them using lots of open-ended questions. Really get to know them. After all, these candidates are the ones most responsible for the company's growth and overall prosperity. The organization's future may rest in their hands.

It is also important to interview each finalist for a management or executive position two or more times. I remember that before I was hired for a management position at one company, I was interviewed *six times* by the executive to whom I would report, *twice* by that executive's boss, and *once* by the company's executive recruiter.

When I quipped that I was coming in so often for interviews that perhaps I should camp out at the company or charge them for all the time the multiple interviews were taking, I received a brutally blunt response: If a candidate could not handle the company's rigorous, in-depth selection process, then that person probably would not prove similarly persistent and quality-conscious if hired by the company.

I was eventually hired by this company and found that its highly successful methods did indeed focus heavily on making careful and wise management decisions, and on profiting greatly from such knowledgeable decision making. The company's careful selection process reflected its whole management strategy and business success. Although this company may have gone to extremes, the lesson it taught should be spread through all companies: Give lots of time to management and executive candidates:

- Spend at least two hours per interview.
- Schedule multiple interviews with each finalist.
- Have several executives interview each finalist.
- Cease to consider any candidate who refuses to endure such heavy interviewing as that candidate would probably balk at other high-intensity situations on the job.

Actions to Take During Each Interview

Four actions or steps go into each interview:

1. *Open the interview.* Start by:

- Greeting the candidate with a smile and a handshake
- Using one or two minutes to chat about the weather or traveling in order to ease into the interview
- Offering the candidate coffee, tea, a soft drink, or water

The entire first step should take only two to five minutes. Note how quickly the candidate warms up and begins to feel comfortable. Your observations may help in evaluating the candidate on such job-related criteria as interpersonal skills (e.g., degree of friendliness) or personality traits (e.g., ability to handle stressful situations).

Remember, it is *not* the interviewer's duty to spend a lot of time trying to make the candidate feel good. Indeed, since it is the candidate who is on stage, the interviewer should instead observe how the candidate tries to make the interviewer feel comfortable and positive toward himself or herself.

2. *Collect information.* Start by telling the candidate the four subjects the interview will cover, namely (1) work history, (2) education and training, (3) career goals, and (4) anything else the candidate wants to add.

In this step, you will mainly be collecting information by using the following techniques:

- Ask mainly open-ended questions.
- Probe a lot, especially the candidate's choice or change points.

- Listen carefully for patterns that reflect on the candidate's ability to meet the six to nine job-related criteria listed on the Interview Guide Form.
- Make notes on the Interview Guide Form.

3. *Maintain a spirit of rapport during the interview.* Generally, it proves best *not* to disagree, argue, or show shock with the candidate's answers.

4. *End the interview.* Specifically, tell the candidate what the next steps are in the selection process, for example, who else will be interviewing him or when he may expect a call to return for more interviews. Then thank the candidate for coming to the interview and take him to the door of the building or to the next interviewer.

Traps Set by Applicants

Even interviewers who do a good job analysis, customize an Interview Guide Form, and ask probing open-ended questions may fall into some common traps laid by candidates. Dodging these traps boils down to heeding three *avoid* warnings.

Using the Word We

Don't let them do it. Applicants commonly, sometimes deceptively, overuse the word *we*, as in "*We* planned and implemented such and such a program" or "*We* succeeded in carrying out that assignment." Often this is a truthful statement that a group of people—not just the candidate—did the work. However, the interviewer is not concerned with hiring an entire group. The interviewer needs only to resolve whether or not to hire the one individual candidate who is being interviewed.

So, it often proves necessary to tell candidates politely to refrain from using the word *we*. When a candidate says *We*, in a context that makes it hard to discern specifically what the candidate did, the interviewer can say:

I understand that you did this project with other people. However, I'm particularly interested in what

you did on the project you are describing. So, please
tell me what *you* did, use the word *I,* and, except when
absolutely necessary, avoid using the word *we.*

The candidate may respond that a group or team really did
do the project. When this occurs, the interviewer can reply:

I appreciate that fact. However, I need to get to know
you and what *you* did. So, please use the word *I* most
of the time and refrain from using the word *we.*

Offering Generalities

Don't let them get away with it. Pin them down. Candidates
often gloss over the specifics of what they did on a job or project.
Instead, they offer generalities, such as, "I succeeded in imple-
menting the such and such program." Naive interviewers often
accept at face value that the candidate is successful or results-
oriented. However, a more astute interviewer will realize that
this generality may not tell the whole story. For instance, how
specifically did the candidate implement the program? And did
the program achieve its goals?

The prescription to get candidates beyond generalities and
into specifics is this: When an applicant gives a generality, follow up with open-ended probes:

"Tell me specifically what you did."
"Give me some examples of how you implemented the
   program."
"Explain exactly how you managed to do that."
"I'd like to hear about the results of the program in detail."

Giving Only Positive Answers

Be cynical about candidates who appear too perfect, too
gung ho. Of course, every outstanding job prospect has done a
lot of wonderful things. However, some applicants artfully
phrase every response in glowing, positive terms. While they
may be telling the truth for the most part, a shrewd interviewer

will realize that any negative information is being downplayed. If a well-rehearsed candidate faces an overly trusting interviewer, that interviewer may never uncover how human—with all the weaknesses that implies—the candidate really is. To avoid falling into this trap, you could ask the overly positive-talking candidate questions like this:

> "You described your success on that project. What problems did you encounter?"
> "What did you not do as well as you might have?"
> "In retrospect, what would have been an even better way of carrying out that assignment?"
> "Tell me about a time you goofed up. Describe it in detail."

After asking such questions, you can then observe whether the applicant's answers meet such job-related criteria as:

- Being candid or open in discussing problems
- Being detail-focused
- Being able to handle stress

Meeting With the Interviewers Who Interviewed Each Candidate

After all the finalists for a position have been interviewed, all those who interviewed them must hold a meeting to come to a final decision. The candidates and ratings of the candidates should be discussed in this meeting. The outcome is a decision or consensus about which finalist is most likely to succeed on the job. That applicant can then be offered the position.

These meetings choose the company's future employees. Nevertheless, office politics sometimes make their presence felt. For instance, the most powerful manager at the meeting may seek to impose his or her opinions on everyone else. Or some participants may evaluate applicants on the basis of *non*job-related criteria.

Despite such wrinkles, the manager to whom the new employee will report must firmly focus the discussion on the six to nine make-or-break job-related criteria. After all, if a below-average or just average candidate gets hired, his or her manager is going to have to live with whatever problems that fact causes. So it definitely pays to run these meetings with an eye toward which applicants could contribute most to productivity and profitability.

The final step at the meeting is to fill in a Candidate Rating Sheet. This sheet is filled in with up-pointing, sideways-pointing, and down-pointing arrows from *each* interviewer to signify how each prediction method, such as interviews, forecasts how the candidate would perform on the job. Let's say that the two final candidates for a salesperson job are Terry Smith and Chris Jones. If both did well on their interviews, then the filled-in Candidate Rating Sheet after the interviews would look like the one shown in Exhibit 3-4.

The Candidate Rating Sheet in Exhibit 3-4 shows that both interviewers were impressed by the two candidates. As a result, both candidates earned up arrows from the interviewers. Their arrow ratings for tests and reference checks can be filled in only after the candidates go through those two prediction methods. This will be shown in Chapters 4 and 5 for tests and in Chapter 6 for reference checks.

Legal Guidelines in Interviewing

The basic guideline in interviewing is to be sure that only legally justifiable questions are asked of applicants.* If interviewers keep this simple rule in mind, they can avoid scores of potential minefields. The key guideline is the following: *Ask only job-related questions.*

In Chapter 1, I boiled down the essential legalities of all hiring decisions to four key points. Specifically, to be legal, the methods used in evaluating applicants must be:

---

*Although this book presents some important legal guidelines, it is not intended to supply all legal information an organization might need. Each organization should confer with an employment law attorney when it needs legal advice on its particular employment practices or problems.

Exhibit 3-4.   Candidate Rating Sheet filled in after interviews with two candidates, Terry Smith and Chris Jones.

	Candidates	
Prediction Methods	Terry Smith	Chris Jones
Interviewer 1	↑	↑
Interviewer 2	↑	↑
Tests		
Reference checks		

1. Job-related
2. Valid
3. Reliable
4. Used by the organization in a nondiscriminatory manner

Here's how to follow these four guidelines when interviewing and what to keep at the top of your mind.

Job-Relatedness

To be within the law, it is crucial for you to ask only job-related questions in an interview. From a purely practical perspective, as well, the most important factor to focus on while hiring is how well the candidate will carry out his or her job-related duties. As such, asking job-related questions not only fulfills the requirements of the law, it also helps you to pinpoint how well a candidate will perform if hired.

Many managers, however, can't seem to resist asking *non*job-related questions. There's a reason for this. Managers are eager to know how candidates' nonwork-related concerns may affect their work productivity. Fortunately, there are ways to get at these issues without asking nonwork-oriented questions.

For instance, a concern commonly expressed by managers is that an applicant may have small children. They worry that caring for those children might cause the applicant to miss work, arrive late, leave early, or quit the job suddenly if she or he finds it hard or impossible to make appropriate child-care arrangements.

However important this concern may be, it is *not* legal to ask, "Do you have well-established child-care arrangements?" Why? Because the question is not *directly* related to the applicant's ability to do the job.

By contrast, it *is* job-related for a manager to ask the same applicant, "What sort of difficulties, if any, would you see in working our regular office hours, putting in occasional overtime, and at times doing some overnight traveling?"

A manager also could say, "If you get this job, your regular work hours would be 8:00 A.M. until 4:30 P.M. Can you *always* work those hours?"

Another concern managers have is whether someone with a noticeable disability—for example, a person in a wheelchair—can carry out the required job duties. It is *not* job-related to say, "I see you're in a wheelchair. Since walking may be difficult or impossible for you, can you do this job?" Of course, the answer to this question is exactly what the interviewer wants and needs to know.

However, the same information can be pursued by means of this job-related inquiry: "In this job, you need to carry out X, Y, and Z job duties. Can you perform those duties?" If the candidate says that the disability would hinder such activities, the interviewer can decide (1) this fact rules out the candidate from further consideration for job-related reasons, or (2) the job could be redesigned so as to enable the candidate to be hired but not required to perform certain duties normally pertaining to that job.

Exhibit 3-5 gives an array of ready-to-use pointers that help interviewers fulfill the requirements of the law during interviews. While a cursory glance may lead you to believe that a manager's hands are tied concerning many questions, a closer review reveals a pattern that managers should be able to live with.

Specifically, the essence of questions that are not allowed is that they are *not* directly related to whether the applicant can do the job. Furthermore, the allowed questions (shown in the right-hand column) permit you to ask the candidate about qualities that can lead to job success. So, rather than feeling op-

(text continues on page 61)

Exhibit 3-5. Legal guidelines for interviewing.

Subject	Nonjob-Related Questions You Should Not Ask	Job-Related Questions You Can Ask
Age	"How old are you?" "What's your birth date?"	Age-related questions are allowed in signing up a new-hire for benefits.
Arrests	"Have you ever been arrested?"	None. (Reason: Arrests are *not* convictions and may not even relate to the job.)
Convictions	"Have you been convicted of any illegal activities?"	"You applied for the job of cashier. Have you ever been convicted of stealing?" "You applied for the doorman job. Have you ever been convicted of any assault-related charges?"
Handicaps	"I can see you have a disability. Can you do this job?"	"This job would require you to carry out X, Y, and Z duties. Can you perform those duties? Would you need any special accommodations to enable you to perform those duties?"
Gender	"Almost all our employees are men. Are you sure you would feel com-	None allowed unless there is a bona fide occupational qualification

(continues)

Exhibit 3-5   *(continued)*

Subject	Nonjob-Related Questions You Should Not Ask	Job-Related Questions You Can Ask
	fortable in this environment?"	(BFOQ) for the job requiring a person of a particular sex, e.g., modeling women's clothing.
Family	No questions about applicant's family are allowed. "How many children do you have?"	"Can you work such and such hours?"
Marital Status	None allowed. "Have you ever been married?"	"Can you work such and such hours?"
Child Care Arrangements	None allowed. "Is your child in an all-day nursery school?"	"Can you work such and such hours?"
Education	No questions allowed about school connections to specific racial, ancestral, national, or religious groups.	You may ask about degrees earned, training completed related to work, or education-related accomplishments.
Race	None allowed.	None allowed.
Ancestry or National Origin	None allowed.	"To do this job, you must be able to speak Spanish. How well do you speak that language?"
Citizenship	No questions allowed about applicant's specific	"Can you legally work in this country?"

Subject	Nonjob-Related Questions You Should Not Ask	Job-Related Questions You Can Ask
	country of citizenship. "Are you a U.S. citizen?"	
Military Duty	No questions about type of discharge are allowed.	You may ask about what jobs applicant held during his/her military service and whether applicant has any remaining military obligations that could affect the ability to do the job.
Memberships	No questions allowed about non-work-related organizations, such as religious or ethnic groups.	"Do you belong to your professional association?" "What trade groups do you belong to?" "What union, if any, do you belong to?"

pressed by what you should not ask, you should feel free to ask any questions that help reveal the essence of a job candidate: Can this person really do the job?

Validity

The validity of an interview is judged by how well it enables the interviewer to predict accurately how the candidate will perform on the job. A high degree of accuracy constitutes its validity.

Unfortunately, large-scale research shows that most interviewers are absolutely awful at predicting job performance.[2] In other words, the average interviewer might just as well flip a coin to decide on whom to hire—so low is the predictive validity of the typical interview.

And here's the rub. When a court case arises concerning the screening process, it becomes necessary for a company to justify *all* its screening techniques as being valid. This is hard to do with interviews, since most interviews are basically subjective and do not lead to accurate predictions. So, many managers and interviewers could be "up the creek without a paddle" if they have to defend their hiring decisions solely on the basis of subjective interviews for which they possess no proof of any validity.[3]

Fortunately, there are specific interviewing techniques that make the prospects a lot less bleak. Researchers have found that *highly structured interviews can lead to quite accurate predictions of job performance.*[4] In fact, together with my fellow industrial psychologist John J. Seres, I have developed a structured interviewing technique using scorable selection interviews.[5] These interviews and their scoring are so structured that they are essentially verbally given tests. Unfortunately, very few companies ever spend the time and money needed to develop such highly valid scorable interviews. However, use of a fairly structured interview method, such as that shown in this chapter, can lead to much greater accuracy in predictions of performance on the job.

Reliability

Did you and a colleague ever have this experience? You both interviewed the same candidate, but when it came to comparing notes, it sounded as if you were talking about two different people. That's an example of how unreliable interviews can be.

A reliable interview is one in which everyone interviewing the candidate reaches the same conclusions and ratings. For instance, if friendliness is an important component of a job, then every manager who interviews a candidate should come to the same conclusions about how friendly—or unfriendly—the applicant is. That would show reliability on interviewers' ratings of candidate friendliness.

Earlier I stated that most interviews show low validity or accuracy in predicting how applicants will perform on the job. Part of the validity problem stems from the low interview reliability. After all, if two interviewers both interview the same candidate but come to different ratings, then one or both interviewers have arrived at inaccurate or low validity ratings. So, with one or both interviewers arriving at inaccurate findings, the overall validity of the interview is lowered.

To understand this link between low reliability and low validity, think of going to a food store to buy produce. You want to buy only one pound. So, you choose your produce and weigh it. Of course, you want the scale to show a valid (accurate) weight. Let's say that the first scale you use shows your produce weighing exactly one pound. However, if you put your produce on another scale and it indicates that you have 1.5 pounds, the discrepancy necessarily implies (1) the weighing provided by the scales is unreliable, since each scale displayed a different weight for your produce; and (2) with unreliable weighings, you cannot tell which weight is valid or whether either scale gives an accurate (valid) reading.

Because a court challenge to a company's interview procedure would necessitate looking at the interview reliability, it would be best if every interviewer gave coinciding ratings on each candidate.

The key way to improve interview reliability is to train each interviewer so well in evaluating candidates that all interviewers will rate each candidate the same (up, down, or sideways arrows) on both:

1. Each of the job's six to nine job-related criteria
2. Overall candidate rating

Unfortunately, this proves difficult to do for two reasons. First, it is hard to train any group of people to rate *every* candidate *the same.* Second, it is common for even well-trained interviewers to revert to their old, unreliable evaluation methods as time elapses since they attended an interviewing skills workshop.

Nevertheless, in Chapters 2 and 3, you saw methods that can help improve the reliability of ratings based on interview findings. For starters, a good Interview Guide Form, listing factors to look for on each job-related criterion, helps prompt (encourage) each interviewer to focus on the *same* evaluation factors (for an example, see Exhibit 2-7). As such, that could help interviewers rate each candidate appropriately on each job-related criterion.

Also, when multiple interviewers of the same job candidates meet to discuss the candidates, they often get "in sync" about how they rate candidates on (1) each criterion and (2) overall rating. This "inter-rater" agreement or "inter-interviewer" synchronicity improves reliability. Then, the question becomes: Did the interviewers accurately (validly) evaluate each candidate? That question arises because all interviewers can agree on ratings (i.e., have high reliability), but still be rating candidates inaccurately (i.e., have low validity).

As you (the reader) will notice, the elements entailed in assuring reliable *and* valid interview ratings are numerous and often hard to control. Such problems explain why:

- Structured interviews are more likely to yield reliable and valid interview ratings of candidates than unstructured or loosely structured interviews.
- Holding meetings of multiple interviewers after each interviewing go-around (after they all interview the same applicants) helps increase the reliability of ratings, though does not necessarily improve validity.
- More companies use tests, developed using rigorous research, that have built-in high-levels of both reliability and validity. Chapters 4 and 5 discuss tests.

Nondiscriminatory

Managers who make sure their interviews are job-related, valid, and reliable need to add three more ingredients to their interviewing game plan to make sure their interviews are non-discriminatory.

1. Make sure you ask fairly similar questions to each applicant for a job. To put this another way, avoid asking questions to members of certain groups that you do not ask to members of other groups. For instance, an interviewer should not ask certain questions to male applicants that the interviewer does not ask female candidates.

2. When an interviewer rates each candidate after an interview, the interviewer must make certain the rating is based on the same job-related criteria for all applicants, regardless of what groups the applicant may belong to. Following the methods prescribed in this book (in Chapters 2 and 3) makes this easy to do. After all, the customized Interview Guide Form made for each job lists factors to consider when you evaluate a candidate on each job-related criterion.

Exhibit 3-6.   How to conduct great interviews: a checklist.

_____   Use Job Analysis Checklist to pinpoint the top six to nine make-it-or-break-it job-related attributes someone must have to succeed in the job.
_____   Design customized Interview Guide Form.
_____   Make sure each interviewer uses a copy of the same Interview Guide Form for the specific job.
_____   Interview each candidate
     _____   Using mostly open-ended questions
     _____   Covering the four key topics of
          _____   Work history
          _____   Education and training
          _____   Career goals or aspirations
          _____   Other comments or questions the candidate may have
     _____   While taking notes on the Interview Guide Form.
_____   Give arrow ratings (up, sideways, or down) to each candidate immediately following the interview.
_____   Discuss each candidate in a meeting of all the people who have interviewed the applicants.
_____   Fill in Candidate Rating Sheet.

---

3. When every interviewer meets to discuss each candidate, the discussion should focus on how well each individual applicant can or cannot carry out the job-related criteria. Applicants' group membership should not play a role in discussions of how likely it is for an applicant to succeed or fail on the job.

All in all, by interviewing and evaluating each applicant equally and fairly, interviewers probably would be using interviews in a nondiscriminatory manner to help them hire the best.

Chapter 3 has examined how to conduct interviews of job candidates. It covered many steps and techniques. Exhibit 3-6 provides a summary checklist of how to do great interviews.

Notes

1. Michael W. Mercer, *How Winners Do It: High Impact People Skills for Your Career Success* (Winnetka, Ill.: Wellington Publishers, 1989), pp. 49–51.
2. John E. Hunter and Rhonda F. Hunter, "Validity and Utility of Alternative Predictors of Job Performance," *Psychological Bulletin*, Vol. 96, No. 1, 1984, p. 90.
3. Edward B. Mitchell, *To Test or Not to Test: Legal Considerations in Employment Testing* (Cincinnati: Thompson, Hine and Flory, 1992), p. 3.
4. Michael A. Campion, Elliott D. Pursell, and Barbara K. Brown, "Structured Interviewing: Raising the Psychometric Properties of the Employment Interview," *Personnel Psychology,* Spring 1988, p. 25.
5. Michael W. Mercer and John J. Seres, "Using Scorable Interview 'Tests' in Hiring," *Personnel,* June 1987, pp. 57–60.

4

Tests for Predicting Applicants' Job Success

Part I: Tests That Forecast Candidates' On-the-Job Behavior, Mental Abilities, and Character

Preemployment testing helps employers to obtain highly accurate predictions of how applicants are likely to perform on the job. Why? Fully developed preemployment tests are the result of years of scientific research. This research results in objective, valid, and reliable questionnaires.

In contrast, the predictions companies make about candidates on the basis of typically subjective interviews and reference checks possess no verifiable validity or reliability. This proves crucial in two ways. First, any applicant prediction method—interviews, reference checks, or tests—must be valid and reliable to yield accurate predictions about candidates. Second, legal guidelines confirm that potentially justifiable or defensible candidate screening procedures should possess documented validity and reliability. Given these twin needs, it seems obvious why increasing numbers of employers are using tests as an integral part of their preemployment evaluation of job candidates.[1]

Three types of tests that can be used to predict the suitability of candidates for a job are:

1. Behavior tests
2. Mental abilities tests
3. Character tests

This chapter explains and illustrates these three types of tests and shows how managers can use them to hire the best. It also explains how to choose the right tests for your purposes, how to administer them, and how to know what scores to look for.

Choosing the Right Tests

Before you can find suitable preemployment tests, you must first pinpoint the key job-related criteria that candidates must meet to succeed on the job. These criteria may include job-related behaviors, mental abilities, and character qualities. Then choose a test or tests that show whether, or to what degree, candidates have the characteristics desired.

Make sure that the tests selected have been thoroughly researched specifically for preemployment testing of job applicants. Why? Many "tests" or questionnaires are not meant for preemployment testing. Instead, they are intended for the training or teambuilding of current employees (not applicants) or for detecting mental health problems. Therefore, you *must make sure that the tests chosen are specifically developed and validated for testing job candidates.*

After locating potentially suitable job-related tests, you would be wise to ask the test publisher three crucial questions:

1. *What are the statistical research results on the test's reliability and validity?* A properly developed test should have both reliability and validity results that are significant at the $p < .05$ level or better. Such statistics were explained in Chapter 1.

2. *Who from the test publishers' organization will help you to use the tests properly?* Some tests sold through catalogs employ secretaries or salespeople (sometimes glorified by the title "account executives") to advise test buyers. However, because testing is a

rather technical matter, it is preferable for managers to have direct access to a Ph.D.-level industrial psychologist or other highly trained testing expert who handles test development and validation research. Be sure to ask this industrial psychologist or other professional about his or her education, training, and practical experience that could establish this professional as a preemployment test expert. Do this just as you would ask a physician about his or her expertise before using that professional's services. Access to such a professional helps ensure compliance with many technical aspects of test use.

3. *Who administers the tests and where are they scored?* Companies increasingly prefer to use tests that they can administer themselves in the company's own offices. Also, many companies like tests that can be scored immediately after a candidate fills them out. Such on-site scoring could be done by hand or computer. On-site scoring speeds up the candidate evaluation procedure. It is definitely faster than mailing or faxing filled-out tests to a test publisher's office for scoring.

Administering the Tests

Preemployment tests are easy to administer, but they must be administered uniformly. If you want candidates to fill out the tests correctly and fairly, follow this approach:

- Read the test-giving instructions printed in the test's *Administration Manual*.
- Always follow the test-giving instructions with every candidate, never varying how you give the test.
- State the time limits, if any, the candidate has for completing the test.
- Give specific verbal directions to the applicant taking the test.
- In addition, make sure that the candidate fills out the test in a quiet place and with no help or advice from other people on how to answer test questions.

Four Ways of Pinpointing Test Scores That Predict Success on the Job

To profit from the tests, managers must of course first pinpoint what test scores—or patterns or profiles of scores—indicate that a candidate probably will do well on the job if hired. There are four main methods that can help you to decide on the test scores to look for when using preemployment tests:

1. Concurrent validity study
2. Predictive validity study
3. National norms
4. Armchairing, or Delphi Method

The first two methods, concurrent validity study and predictive validity study, both focus on showing preference for applicants whose scores are similar to those of company employees who are high achievers on the job.

In both cases, an already validated test must be used. Then the study uncovers what test scores average, above-average, or excellent employees tend to score. It is important for the company's management to decide how it defines success on the job. Generally, it is preferable to define success by measurable, quantifiable factors. Two typical quantitative gauges are the incumbents' productivity and tenure.

When possible, below-average or low-achieving employees should also be used in the study. In practice, this does not always prove possible because many underachievers quit or are terminated. So, few—if any—below-average employees may be available for the study.

Concurrent Validity Studies

To do a concurrent validity study with current employees, preferably there should be ten or more (preferably more!) high achievers in the same job. If they exist, then follow these steps:

1. Test the high achievers and, if available, also the underachievers.

2. To pinpoint the "success pattern" or profile of the high achievers, use statistics, for example, the "66 percent rule" ("2/3 rule") or analysis of variance or t-test statistics.

The "66 percent rule" is the easiest for managers to use because it requires just looking at simple percentages. This method is used to specify where 66 percent or more of the high achievers tend to score on each test. This is the success pattern of scores for the high achievers. If underachievers are tested too, you can also pinpoint where 66 percent or more of the underachievers typically score. Then the company can show preference for people who score similarly to the high achievers, since this is the success pattern of test scores for their most successful employees.

Exhibit 4-1 shows how such "66 percent rule" calculations can be done using a test that predicts both behaviors and mental abilities. The right-hand side of this exhibit shows the percentage of high achievers who scored within the success pattern parentheses shown in the table's center section. Similar calculations could be made on the same company's underachievers if they too were tested. It is then interesting to see in what ways the high achievers and underachievers score similarly to each other and in what ways they score differently from each other. There usually is overlap between the two groups on some test scales. However, there also tend to be test scales on which the high achievers' scores are quite unlike those of their underachieving counterparts.

One way to pinpoint where high achievers in a particular job score on a test is to:

- Test current employees in that job who are high achievers (and, if available, underachievers, too).
- See where 66 percent or more of the high achievers score within five or six points of each other.
- Indicate with parentheses the "success pattern" for the scores 66 percent or more of the high-achievers got on the test

Exhibit 4-1.   Example of "66 percent rule" calculations for a salesperson's job.

Salesperson at XYZ Company
JOB TITLE

BEHAVIOR FORECASTER™												

												% High Achievers Scoring in Parentheses
Accuracy of this Person's Behavior Forecaster™ Results												
Inaccurate	1	2	3	4	5	(6	7	8	9	10	11)	Accurate 100%
Did this person follow all instructions?												YES / NO

Interpersonal Style												
Unfriendly	1	2	3	4	5	(6	7	8	9	10)	11	Friendly 82%
Passive	1	2	3	4	5	(6	7	8	9	10)	11	Aggressive 90%
Prefers solo work	1	2	(3	4	5	6	7)	8	9	10	11	Prefers teamwork 68%

Personality												
Lax in following rules, policies, & procedures	1	2	3	(4	5	6	7	8)	9	10	11	Rigidly follows rules, policies, & procedures 74%
Emotionally sensitive	1	2	3	4	5	6	(7	8	9	10	11)	Emotionally objective 84%
Pessimistic	1	2	3	4	5	6	(7	8	9	10	11)	Optimistic 90%
Low anxiety	1	2	3	4	(5	6	7	8	9)	10	11	High anxiety 66%
Feeling-focused	1	2	3	4	5	6	7	8	9	10	11	Fact-focused

Motivations												
Not money-motivated	1	2	3	4	5	6	(7	8	9	10	11)	Money-motivated 84%
Not helping-people-motivated	1	2	3	4	(5	6	7	8	9)	10	11	Helping-people-motivated 76%
Not creativity-motivated	1	2	3	4	5	6	7	8	9	10	11	Creativity-motivated
Not power-motivated	1	2	3	4	5	6	(7	8	9	10	11)	Power-motivated 88%
Not knowledge-motivated	1	2	3	4	5	6	7	8	9	10	11	Knowledge-motivated

ABILITIES FORECASTER™												
Low reasoning ability	1	2	3	4	(5	6	7	8	9)	10	11	Strong reasoning ability 76%
Low vocabulary ability	1	2	3	4	5	(6	7	8	9	10)	11	Strong vocabulary ability 66%
Low arithmetic ability	1	2	3	(4	5	6	7	8)	9	10	11	Strong arithmetic ability 88%
Low grammar, spelling, & word use ability	1	2	3	4	(5	6	7	8	9)	10	11	Strong grammar, spelling, & word use ability 76%
Low small detail speed & accuracy ability	1	2	3	(4	5	6	7	8)	9	10	11	Strong small detail speed & accuracy ability 84%

© 1991 MERCER SYSTEMS, INC.

Source: Michael W. Mercer, *Abilities and Behavior Forecaster™ Tests* (Chicago: Mercer Systems, Inc., 1991).

In Exhibit 4-1, the "success pattern" for the high achievers in this specific job in XYZ Company are shown with parentheses. The percentage of high achievers who scored in the parentheses on each test scale is shown in the right-hand column under the heading, "% High Achievers Scoring in Parentheses." For example, 82 percent of the high achievers in this job scored 6 to 10 on the test's Friendliness scale. Since the high achievers did not always have 66 percent or more score within five or six points of each other on certain scales (e.g., Creativity-Motivated), no "success pattern" parentheses was put on those scales.

To help the company hire the best, it should prefer candidates who score in the success pattern parentheses, that is, candidates who score similar to employees who have proven successful on this job at XYZ Company.

In terms of what managers should do, the most important thing is to show preference for candidates who score similarly to the high achievers' success pattern of test scores. For instance, managers at XYZ Company should endeavor to hire sales candidates who score in the success pattern shown in Exhibit 4-1 and who also get positive ratings (up-pointing arrows) on both their interviews and reference checks.

If the easy-to-use "66 percent rule" is not used, then more complex statistics could be calculated to see how a group of high achievers and a group of underachievers score differently on a test. For instance, statistics such as analysis of variance or t-tests could be done to spot statistically significant differences between a group of high achievers and a group of underachievers in the same job. Since most managers are unacquainted with or unversed in these fairly complicated statistics, however, they either do not use them or they must contract with an industrial psychologist to make the calculations.

It is interesting to note, incidentally, that a variation of a concurrent validity study can be done even when few employees work on a particular job. For instance, this may work suitably when pinpointing the cutoff score for a typing test. In a typing test, a candidate is given material to type that is similar to what an employee would have to type on the job. The question that must be answered is "What is a suitable score on the typing test, in terms of the number of words correctly typed or the number of errors made?"

To find an answer to this question, a company can do three things:

1. Get some of its best typists to take the typing test.
2. See how these typists score on the test.
3. Use these good typists' average score as a cutoff score expected from candidates on the typing test, *or* use the lowest score in this group as the cutoff score.

By doing this, there is no single "passing" score for the typing test that would hold good for every organization. Good typists in one company may type forty words per minute. However, good typists in a different organization may type seventy words per minute. What counts is the typing speed needed to do well in a specific job in a particular company. By carrying out the three-step, small-scale concurrent validity study described here, each organization can set its test cutoff scores to reflect the actual job-related skill level needed to succeed in that organization.

Predictive Validity Studies

Doing a predictive validity study differs in one key way from doing a concurrent validity study. In the predictive study, you follow these steps:

1. Test all applicants for a specific job, but do not use these test results in any way in hiring or other management decisions.
2. About a year later, rank everyone hired from top to bottom (high to low) in terms of their success on the job.
3. Compare how the top employees scored on the test with how the bottom employees scored.
4. Then use either the "66 percent rule" or statistics such as analysis of variance or t-tests.

As with the concurrent validity study, you should then show preference for hiring candidates who score similar to the high achievers' success pattern of scores.

While the predictive study can provide a great, scientific way of pinpointing test scores that predict success on the job, it is not used nearly as often as the concurrent study. The reason for this is that most companies that decide to start using tests want to begin soon after making that decision. While the concurrent study can often be completed in just one to four weeks (after which the company can start using the tests in its hiring process), the predictive validity study often takes a year or even longer. Most companies, except for some very large ones, do not want to wait that long to start using preemployment tests to help them hire the best.

National Norms

National norms are the third technique used to decide what test scores may predict job success. This tactic relies on seeing how people in basically the same job in a variety of organizations tend to score on the same test. For example, the national norms for secretaries may be used when hiring secretaries. In fact, for clerical jobs, some research indicates that this method works well.[2]

However, a practical problem may arise when using national norms for a particular type of job. Specifically, a manager could ask:

> Is the average of all the people thrown into the national norms similar to the average successful employee in *my* company? If I use national norms for salespeople, are those norms similar to those of the typical good salespeople in *my* company? Or, if I use national norms for secretaries, will those national benchmarks help me hire secretaries likely to do well in *my* organization?

For instance, let's say a company's top-notch salespeople tend to be extremely friendly and also highly assertive. What happens if the company uses national norms for a behavior test for salespeople in their type of business and those norms indicate that good salespeople should be just average in friendliness and only moderately assertive? While such averages may work out well for a broad cross section of companies, they would not help that manager hire really top people.

Or, let's look at national norms for secretaries. Perhaps the successful secretaries at this manager's company have certain mental abilities, such as above-average vocabulary and grammar skills, similar to those of the large sample of secretaries used to create a mental abilities test's national norms.

However, let's say that this manager's best secretaries also excel at certain job-related behaviors, such as (1) greeting customers (requiring lots of friendliness) and (2) making collections (necessitating a high level of assertiveness). What should this manager do if the national averages on a behavior test show that the norm for secretaries is to have (1) only moderate friendliness (not as useful for greeting customers) and (2) low assertiveness (rather ineffective for doing collections on unpaid bills)? Such national norms on a behavior test would not help that manager to hire highly productive secretaries.

All in all, national norms are sometimes suitable to use and perhaps interesting to examine. However, they may not be as useful as doing a concurrent or predictive study of employees who really are successful at a specific job in a particular company. So, what can a manager do when there are not enough employees in a specific job to make it possible to do a concurrent or predictive study or when the manager does not want to use national norms? This leads to the final technique for figuring out what test scores to look for in potentially productive candidates.

Armchairing

This fourth technique is also known as the Delphi Method. Armchairing requires two managers familiar with the job for which tests will be used to sit down together (in armchairs, so to speak) to discuss the attributes of successful employees in that job.

They look at a list of the job-related criteria or "scales" the test will measure, such as various interpersonal skills, mental abilities, or other attributes, and then decide how someone who would be successful in the job would tend to score on these scales. Then, the test scores pinpointed by these two managers can be used as benchmarks against which to rate each applicant for the job. Interestingly, when two managers who really know a job do armchairing, they invariably arrive at very similar conclusions as to the test scores they would expect a high achiever to obtain.

It should be pointed out that armchairing is not as scientific as the three other methods discussed. In fact, armchairing is somewhat like managers coming up with a list of job-related criteria to look for in a job interview. The major difference is that whereas the interview ratings may be rather subjective, at least the test scores derive from objectively validated tests. So, armchairing is at least more objective than the typical interview in terms of rating candidates on job-related criteria.

Three Types of Preemployment Tests to Predict a Candidate's Behavior, Mental Abilities, and Character

The following sections of this chapter provide overviews of three types of test, their practical uses, and give examples of how they are set up and how they work.

Behavior Tests

These tests, composed of multiple-choice questions, predict how someone will behave on the job. They typically examine three crucial aspects of work behavior:

1. Interpersonal skills
2. Personality traits
3. Motivations

Because these tests do not have any "right" or "wrong" answers in the usual sense, they are sometimes called questionnaires rather than tests.

Exhibit 4-2.   Questions that must be answered when choosing a test to predict candidates' on-the-job behavior.

Question 1.   What behaviors (interpersonal skills, personality traits, and motivations) are needed to succeed on the job for which the behavior test will be used?

2.   What behavior test measures or predicts those behaviors?

3.   Was the behavior test developed and validated specifically for workplace testing?

4.   Does the test possess a scale that would detect a candidate who tried to fake it? That is, can the test ferret out an applicant who gears his answers to what he believes is desirable in a candidate—but not necessarily true of himself?

When choosing a behavior test to predict job behavior, managers must first answer the four key questions appearing in Exhibit 4-2.

The first question in the exhibit has to do with determining the types of interpersonal skills, personality traits, and motivations that are needed to succeed on the job. Research shows that behavior tests can have high predictive validity when a manager first figures out what behaviors are relevant to test and then chooses a test that inquires into those job-related criteria.[3]

Doing a job analysis of what it takes to succeed on the job leads the manager into asking the second question: What test measures those behaviors? For example, let's suppose you are a sales manager who notices that the company's most successful salespeople are (1) highly assertive, (2) extraordinarily optimistic, and (3) very driven to earn big commission checks. In this case, you should definitely seek a behavior test that measures (1) interpersonal skills such as assertiveness, (2) personality traits such as optimism, and (3) motivations such as money motivation. Only by finding such a test can you measure these crucial job-related behaviors.

Whether the behavior test was developed and validated specifically for workplace testing is a very significant point. Most behavior or personality tests are developed for clinical or mental health testing—*not* for workplace testing. Thus, when you are seeking a suitable test, you may find an array of clinical or mental health tests that assess some job-relevant criteria but that also measure such nonjob-related criteria as neurosis, hypochondria, schizophrenia, paranoia, or other mental disorders. These tests were neither developed nor meant for testing job candidates.

There are two methods for avoiding choosing a clinical test. First, look at the scales or behaviors the test measures. Are they relevant to workplace behavior? Second, ask if the test was developed for workplace testing by means of research on people who work full-time. Many tests are developed by university professors of psychology who use college freshmen as research subjects when developing tests. Most businesses, however, are more concerned with hiring working adults than with hiring college freshmen. Thus, it is more relevant to choose a test whose research focused on working adults.

Finally, you need to know whether a candidate can fake any part of the behavior test. That is, could applicants answer in such a way that they come across as better or different than they really are? For instance, could a candidate fake his answers so that the test results would show him to be friendlier or more teamwork-oriented than he really is?

Fortunately, properly developed behavior tests *always* contain a scale geared to uncover a candidate who tries to come across differently or better than he or she really is. Such scales on the test may be labeled:

- Accuracy scale
- Distortion scale
- Validity scale

Regardless of what the scale is called, the technique used to uncover candidates who try to fake out a test is the same. They are uncovered by interspersing "truism" questions throughout the questionnaire. These truism questions, taken together, form the foundation for the accuracy, distortion, validity, or "faking good" scale. Exhibit 4-3 shows two examples of a particular behavior test's numerous truism questions composing the test's accuracy scale.[4]

For example, it is a truism for virtually every person that

Exhibit 4-3. Questions designed to detect if a job candidate is trying to "fake good" on a behavior test.

Some people are friendlier to me than I am to them.

           1. Yes   2. Uncertain   3. No

I have said things behind someone's back that I would not say to that person's face.

           1. Yes   2. Uncertain   3. No

Source: Michael W. Mercer, *Behavior Forecaster*™ *Test* (Chicago: Mercer Systems, Inc., 1991), pp. 2 and 3.

"some people are friendlier to me than I am to them." Very few people could sincerely answer no to that statement. However, a candidate trying to fake good might do so.

The next example given in the exhibit is a truism to which 99.999 percent of the population should answer yes. After all, it is hard to find someone who has not "said things behind someone's back that I would not say to that person's face." Nevertheless, an applicant who aims to "fake good" or come across better than he or she really is may answer no to that test item.

The candidate's entire accuracy scale score is not dependent on how he answers just these two examples shown in the exhibit. There are, after all, many truism questions on the behavior test. However, if someone answers quite a few of these questions in an "inaccurate" manner, then he would get a low score on the test's accuracy scale. Should this happen, a crucial question arises: If the applicant tried to fake good on the truism questions, did he perhaps try to come across better on other questions too? If this is the case, then the candidate's scores on the remaining behavior test scales may not be an accurate reflection of his behavior on the job. This is not because the test is not valid. Rather, it is because the applicant went through the behavior test trying to fake good and, in doing so, did not candidly reveal his real interpersonal skills, personality traits, and motivations.

Unfortunately, despite the potential for candidates to try to fake good on a behavior or personality test, some managers use questionnaires that do not contain an accuracy, distortion, validity, or other such scale to detect a candidate who tries to fake out the test!! Why do managers make such a profound blunder? What usually happens is that a manager attends a teambuilding or training session at which a "test" or "personality inventory" is administered to all participants. These questionnaires are designed *solely* for teambuilding or training. They are *not* designed, developed, or intended for preemployment testing. For instance, one such inventory classifies people into four personal styles or types. It is fun and nonthreatening to use in teambuilding or training programs.

However, that questionnaire contains no scale to detect a person who tries to fake good! For example, I met one person who took this inventory four times and *purposely* faked out the questionnaire. Each time, he made himself sound like a different one of this questionnaire's four personal styles or types! Since this popular questionnaire contains no scale to detect such faking, nothing in his scores indicated that he had purposely faked out the personality inventory. Any manager who uses such an inventory runs the risk of hiring people who behave on the job very differently from the way that inappropriately chosen questionnaire had indicated they would.

In sum, the rule to follow is to *use only tests specifically developed for preemployment evaluations.* These tests *must* contain a scale to spot applicants who try to come across better than or different from how they really are. Avoid using any test that (1) is not designed for candidate screening or (2) does not contain an accuracy-type scale.

Using a Behavior Test

One particular behavior test predicts a candidate's success on the job in terms of crucial behaviors that can make or break a person's job performance.[5] It predicts or forecasts how an applicant will act on the job on the basis of three patterns:

1. Interpersonal styles
   —Friendliness
   —Assertiveness
   —Teamwork versus solo work preference

2. Personality traits
   —Reaction to rules, policies, and procedures
   —Emotional sensitivity versus objectivity
   —Optimism
   —Anxiety
   —Feeling focus versus fact focus
3. Motivations
   —Money motivation
   —Motivation to help people
   —Creativity motivation
   —Power motivation
   —Knowledge motivation

Exhibit 4-4 shows the success pattern of scores for high-achieving salespeople in Company XYZ. This success pattern derives from a concurrent validity study of Company XYZ's salespeople. Armed with this information, the company can then take the following actions:

- Test candidates for the sales job using this behavior test, an eighty-eight-question test taking fifteen to twenty minutes for an applicant to fill out.
- Score the test on its computer, including inserting the parentheses showing the company's salesperson success pattern.
- Compare each candidate's scores, shown with an X, to the success pattern in parentheses.
- Decide on an arrow rating of the candidate based on the test scores.
- Put the rating on the Candidate Rating Sheet.

For example, let's say that two applicants, Terry Smith and Chris Jones, are being considered for a sales position at this company. Their scores on this behavior test (shown as Xs) and the job's success pattern (shown as parentheses) appear in both Exhibit 4-4 and Exhibit 4-5.

To see how well each of the two candidates fits into this job's success pattern:

(text continues on page 87)

Exhibit 4-4. Behavior test scores of a candidate who scores similar to those of XYZ Company's most productive salespeople.

CANDIDATE: *Terry Smith*	SALESPERSON REPORT

*Accuracy of this Person's **Behavior Forecaster**™ Results*

	1 2 3 4 5 6 7 8 9 10 11	
Inaccurate	(X)	Accurate

Interpersonal Style

	1 2 3 4 5 6 7 8 9 10 11	
Unfriendly	X)	Friendly
Passive	(X)	Aggressive
Prefers solo work	(X)	Prefers teamwork

Personality

	1 2 3 4 5 6 7 8 9 10 11	
Lax in following rules, policies, and procedures	(X)	Rigidly follows rules, policies, and procedures
Emotionally sensitive	(X) ( )	Emotionally objective
Pessimistic	(X)	Optimistic
Has low anxiety	X X)	Has high anxiety
Feeling-focused	X	Fact-focused

(continues)

Exhibit 4-4 *(continued)*

Motivations

	1	2	3	4	5	6	7	8	9	10	11	
Low money motivation				(X							X)	High money motivation
Low helping people motivation						(			)			High helping-people motivation
Low creativity motivation					X							High creativity motivation
Low power motivation						(		X		)		High power motivation
Low knowledge motivation					X		X					High knowledge motivation

Notes: 1. Each X shows where the candidate scored on this test.

2. The "success pattern" parentheses indicate where highly productive salespeople in this company tend to score, according to a study of the company's high-achieving salespeople.

3. Three scales show no "success pattern" parentheses because this company's high-achieving salespeople's test scores showed no definite pattern on those scales. Their scores were scattered across the eleven-point range for scales on Feeling-Focused versus Fact-Focused, Creativity Motivation, and Knowledge Motivation.

4. Circled X indicates where the candidate scored differently from the "success pattern" of the company's high-achieving salespeople.

Source: Michael W. Mercer, *Administration Manual for the Behavior Forecaster™ and Abilities Forecaster™ Tests* (Chicago: Mercer Systems, Inc., 1991), p. 21.

Exhibit 4-5. Behavior test scores of a candidate whose scores differ from those of XYZ Company's most productive salespeople.

CANDIDATE: *Chris Jones*   *SALESPERSON REPORT*

*Accuracy of this Person's **Behavior Forecaster** Results*

	1	2	3	4	5	6	7	8	9	10	11	
Inaccurate						(	X				)	Accurate

Interpersonal Style

	1	2	3	4	5	6	7	8	9	10	11	
Unfriendly				Ⓧ	(					)		Friendly
Passive					(X		X)			)		Aggressive
Prefers solo work	(											Prefers teamwork

Personality

	1	2	3	4	5	6	7	8	9	10	11	
Lax in following rules, policies, and procedures					(		X	)				Rigidly follows rules, policies, and procedures
Emotionally sensitive				Ⓧ		(				)		Emotionally objective
Pessimistic				Ⓧ		(				)		Optimistic
Has low anxiety					(X			)	X			Has high anxiety
Feeling-focused									X			Fact-focused

(continues)

Exhibit 4-5 *(continued)*

Motivations

	1	2	3	4	5	6	7	8	9	10	11	
Low money motivation			(X)				(				)	High money motivation
Low helping-people motivation						(			X)			High helping-people motivation
Low creativity motivation					X							High creativity motivation
Low power motivation						(		X				High power motivation
Low knowledge motivation									X			High knowledge motivation

Notes: 1. Each *X* shows where the candidate scored on this test.

2. The "success pattern" parentheses indicate where highly productive salespeople in this company tend to score, according to a study of the company's high-achieving salespeople.

3. Three scales show no "success pattern" parentheses because this company's high-achieving salespeople's test scores showed no definite pattern on those scales. Their scores were scattered across the eleven-point range for scales on Feeling-Focused vs. Fact-Focused, Creativity Motivation, and Knowledge Motivation.

4. Circled *X*s indicate where the candidate scored differently from the "success pattern" of the company's high-achieving salespeople.

Source: Michael W. Mercer, *Administration Manual for the Behavior Forecaster™ and Abilities Forecaster™ Tests* (Chicago: Mercer Systems, Inc., 1991) p. 23.

- Note where the candidate scores inside the parentheses, that is, whether the person scored similarly to productive employees in this job.
- Circle each score (X) where the applicant scores outside the success pattern parentheses.

First, Terry Smith scored similarly to this job's high achievers on all scales except one. Specifically, Terry has scored three points too low on the emotional sensitivity versus objectivity scale. For that reason, Terry's score of four on that scale suggests that Terry would have a rather hard time taking rejection or criticism.

Next, examine the other candidate's scores. Chris Jones has scored outside the success pattern parentheses on four scales: friendliness, emotional sensitivity versus objectivity, optimism, and money motivation.

Now, giving each candidate an arrow rating based on the person's scores will probably yield the following ratings:

- *Up-pointing arrow for Terry Smith.* Terry warrants this rating because Terry scores outside the success pattern parentheses only once. Also, Terry's one score outside the success pattern is on emotional sensitivity. That is a behavior Terry possibly could learn to change.

- *Down-pointing arrow for Chris Jones.* After all, Chris scores outside the success pattern on quite a few scales. Perhaps with effort Chris could learn to improve on two of the behaviors evaluated by the test. For example, Chris might be able to learn to (1) act in a friendlier fashion and (2) be less emotionally sensitive to criticism or rejection at work. However, Chris also came across as rather pessimistic. Because pessimism is a deeply ingrained personality trait, Chris may find it difficult to change into a more optimistic, can-do type of person. In addition, with a low score (only 3) on money motivation, Chris would feel extremely *de*motivated by this sales job's pay program, which relies heavily on salespeople earning commissions and bonuses by selling large volumes of goods. Chris's below-average money motivation score indicates that Chris would feel quite uncomfortable running after almost any type of incentive pay.

Let's suppose both Terry Jones and Chris Smith did wonderfully in their interviews, as mentioned in Chapter 3. Then the Candidate Rating Sheet would be filled in as shown in Exhibit 4-6. Because hiring employees is based on the laws of probability, Terry appears more likely than Chris to do a good job. The reasons?

- Terry earned all up-pointing arrows, meaning that all predictions on Terry tag this person as a potentially successful employee.
- Although Chris did well in the interviews, this candidate's job behavior as predicted by the validated behavior test indicates that Chris may not have what it takes to succeed in this job in this company.

Mental Abilities Tests

To understand the usefulness of testing candidates' mental abilities, you should answer these questions. Did you ever hire someone and then find out that your new employee has one or more of these problems:

- Seems too dense to do the job or, conversely, is too bright for the job and gets bored rather quickly?
- Misunderstands or misinterprets words while speaking or writing?
- Messes up basic calculations needed to do the job?
- Misspells or writes ungrammatically so that you must

Exhibit 4-6. Candidate Rating Sheet for Terry Smith and Chris Jones.

| | Candidates | |
	Terry Smith	*Chris Jones*
Interviewer #1	↑	↑
Interviewer #2	↑	↑
Behavior test	↑	↓

waste time proofreading this person's memos, letters, reports, or typing?
- Makes costly mistakes when attempting to handle small details quickly?

Unfortunately, most managers would answer yes to one or more of these questions. Such problems illustrate how valuable it is to test candidates' mental abilities to find out about their skills *before* you get stuck with a below-average employee on your payroll. It always pays to hire the best—and this includes hiring employees with the mental abilities required to successfully do all their job-related duties.

Mental abilities tests exist to help evaluate candidates. Abilities typically predicted by these instruments include the following:

- Reasoning or problem solving
- Vocabulary
- Grammar, spelling, and correct use of words
- Arithmetic or computations
- Speed and accuracy in handling small details

Some or all of these abilities are needed in a wide array of jobs.

All the abilities relate in some degree to a person's general level of intelligence. This refers to proficiency in mental tasks that people face in every area of their lives. These proficiencies include understanding problems, figuring out solutions, remembering information, and correctly using information.

Voluminous research shows that predicting intelligence-related abilities plays a key role in hiring employees who are successful on the job. From a purely practical perspective, every experienced manager has had the ill-fortune to hire someone who may have the appropriate interpersonal skills, personality, and motivation to handle a job but who proves not mentally astute enough to carry out the job's requirements. The flip side of the coin is that an employee may have much more intelligence than the job requires, and, as a result, becomes bored by the job.

In addition to what the practical experience of most managers tells us, management professor James Q. Wilson of the University of California at Los Angeles in a review of the book *A Question of Intelligence: The IQ Debate in America* by Daniel Seligman (New York: Carol Publishing [Birch Lane Press], 1992) reports:

> People who mistakenly think that "intelligence is only what intelligence tests test" will be surprised to learn how powerfully IQ predicts not only school achievement but also job performance—even in jobs that don't require people to engage mostly in "mental" activities. Soldiers firing tank guns are more likely to hit their targets if they have higher IQs. Bright police officers make better cops than not-so-bright ones. Professor John E. Hunter of Michigan State concluded after surveying the abundant evidence on this matter that there are *no* jobs for which intelligence tests do not predict performance. Of course other factors, such as personality and work habits, also make a difference, but IQ is emphatically not just a matter of being "good with words."[6]

Given the important role that mental abilities play in a person's ultimate job success—or failure—more and more managers are realizing that being able to validly or accurately predict candidates' aptitudes is crucial to hiring productive employees. For this reason, tests of job-related mental abilities are not only useful but essential to managers.

Using a Mental Abilities Test

One particular preemployment test[7] of mental abilities contains five subtests that predict candidates' aptitudes on the following:

- Reasoning or problem solving
- Vocabulary
- Arithmetic
- Grammar, spelling, and word use
- Small detail speed and accuracy

Like the behavior test, this mental abilities test yields scores on a 1 to 11 continuum. A score of 1 indicates low ability, while a score of 11 shows keen ability. For instance, if someone scores 11 on reasoning, then that person shows a strong ability to understand and solve problems. In contrast, someone scoring 1 on reasoning would find it difficult to grasp problems and figure out correct solutions.

It is important to note that many executives want to have only employees who score high on all mental abilities. Although this may seem to make sense, in reality it does not work well. Why? Because most jobs do not require extremely high levels of mental abilities. Some jobs, like professional and management jobs, are done best by people with strong aptitudes. Most other jobs, however, require more moderate or even fairly low levels of mental abilities.

For instance, I once visited a business where mentally retarded people work. Their intelligence levels were well below average. One woman there works forty hours a week standing next to a conveyor belt. Fruit and vegetables travel down the conveyor belt past this woman. Her job is to look at the produce and remove from the conveyor belt any fruit or vegetable that is bruised or has insects crawling on it.

This retarded woman has worked in the same job and at the same conveyor belt for about twenty years. When I asked her if she ever got bored with her job, she replied in total earnestness, "Of course not, I *never* get bored. Every piece of fruit or vegetable is *different!*"

Most people with average or above-average intelligence would quickly become bored stiff doing that woman's job. However, people with lower-level IQs, such as retarded people have, often find it easier to stay interested in repetitious or rote work. Their mental abilities fit well with the aptitudes needed to successfully do such repetitive tasks—and *not* get bored.

XYZ Company's use of mental abilities tests shows how they work. As described earlier, the concurrent validation study done on XYZ Company's salespeople involved both a behavior test and a mental abilities test. The bottom portion of Exhibit 4-1, given earlier in this chapter, shows the success pattern of mental abilities test scores of the company's top salespeople.

Exhibit 4-7. Mental abilities test scores of candidate Terry Smith.

CANDIDATE: *Terry Smith*   *SALESPERSON REPORT*

	1	2	3	4	5	6	7	8	9	10	11	
Low reasoning ability					(				X)			Strong reasoning ability
Low vocabulary ability					(		X			)		Strong vocabulary ability
Low arithmetic ability				(	X			)				Strong arithmetic ability
Low grammar, spelling, and word use ability					(			X	)			Strong grammar, spelling, and word use ability
Low small-detail speed and accuracy ability				(				X)				Strong small-detail speed and accuracy ability

Source: Michael W. Mercer, *Administration Manual for the Behavior Forecaster™ and Abilities Forecaster™ Tests* (Chicago: Mercer Systems, Inc., 1991), p. 22.

But how did our two candidates, Terry Smith and Chris Jones, do in terms of their mental abilities test results? Their individual scores and the success pattern parentheses for the job appear in Exhibit 4-7 and Exhibit 4-8, respectively.

By scoring in the success pattern parentheses, Terry scored similarly to the company's most productive salespeople. Chris did too. As such, both deserve an up-pointing arrow predicting that their mental abilities will help them to do well on the job. So, up arrows would be put on the Candidate Rating Sheet. Now, after all their interview arrow ratings as well as their ratings on both the behavior test and the mental abilities test are inserted, the rating sheet looks like that in Exhibit 4-9.

If Exhibit 4-9 showed *all* the ratings on these two candidates, then Terry Smith would be the obvious winner. After all, every prediction about Terry is positive. This increases the likelihood that Terry will perform well if hired by the company. By contrast, although Chris Jones receives mostly up arrows, Chris's behaviors—as predicted by the behavior test—indicate that Chris has a lower likelihood of doing well on the job. Chris may be a winner for other jobs, but not for this specific job in this company.

Character Tests

Character tests predict job-related character or integrity factors. These factors may include the following:

- Trustworthiness
- Honesty
- Potential for stealing
- Commitment to work ethic
- Potential for substance abuse

The two types of character questionnaires are (1) confession-based questionnaires and (2) projective attitudes or opinions.

Confession-based tests ask candidates if they have ever committed specific misdeeds, crimes, or other antisocial acts. Such questions may directly ask applicants if they have stolen

Exhibit 4-8. Mental abilities test scores of candidate Chris Jones.

CANDIDATE: *Chris Jones*   *SALESPERSON REPORT*

	1	2	3	4	5	6	7	8	9	10	11	
Low reasoning ability				(		X			)			Strong reasoning ability
Low vocabulary ability				(X						)		Strong vocabulary ability
Low arithmetic ability			(X					)				Strong arithmetic ability
Low grammar, spelling, and word use ability					(		X		)			Strong grammar, spelling, and word ability
Low small-detail speed and accuracy ability			(X					)				Strong small-detail speed and accuracy ability

Source: Michael W. Mercer, *Administration Manual for the Behavior Forecaster™ and Abilities Forecaster™ Tests* (Chicago: Mercer Systems, Inc., 1991), p. 24.

Exhibit 4-9. Candidate Rating Sheet on Terry Smith and Chris Jones.

| | *Candidates* | |
	Terry Smith	Chris Jones
Interviewer #1	↑	↑
Interviewer #2	↑	↑
Behavior test	↑	↓
Mental abilities test	↑	↑

from their employers, used specific drugs, or engaged in other offenses.

While admissions to such acts would obviously prove useful to a prospective employer, confession-based integrity tests unfortunately are (1) easy to fake and (2) potentially invasive of privacy. First, an astute candidate knows enough not to admit to crimes or misconduct. Second, some people consider the questions an invasion of privacy that goes way beyond what an employer should ask. Given these two problems, confession-based tests are falling into disfavor.

As a result, the remaining option for a paper-and-pencil character test is a personality testing technique known as a projective attitude or opinion questionnaire. The questions on this test do not ask candidates directly to admit to or confess improprieties. Instead, applicants are asked their opinions as to how others or people in general would respond to specific situations involving character or integrity choices. The questions, in effect, get candidates to *project* how they themselves would respond.

Using a Character Test

One character test predicts candidates' attitudes toward (1) drinking and taking drugs, (2) honesty and trustworthiness, and (3) alienation from work or their work ethic.[8]

Exhibit 4-10 shows two of the sixty-one questions or items used to predict trustworthiness. Note that each item asks the applicant to project his or her opinions onto other people or

Exhibit 4-10. Sample questions on trustworthiness from a character test.

A. If a person is clever enough to cheat someone out of a large sum of money, he ought to be allowed to keep it.	Yes (?) No
B. There are some circumstances that justify taking money without permission from an employer.	Yes (?) No

Note: (?) means "uncertain."
Source: Robert W. Cormack, *P.A.S.S.-III*® *D.A.T.A.*® *Survey* (Oak Brook, Ill.: Personnel Systems Corporation, 1987).

people in general. They do not ask the candidate to say what he or she has done or might do in such situations.

The character test's scoring yields a risk rating—low, moderate, or high—on each of the three character traits the questionnaire surveys. Of course, companies would prefer to hire candidates who earn low-risk or perhaps moderate-risk ratings on each of the three attributes. A high-risk candidate might be considered if (1) the company needs the applicant's special skills or (2) there is only a very limited choice of candidates.

If you are the manager doing the hiring, you can also use the candidate's survey responses as a basis for interview questions. For instance, let's say that an applicant's answers on the sixty-one trustworthiness items earned her a moderate-risk rating on trustworthiness. Maybe she answered the two trustworthiness items shown in Exhibit 4-10 in a manner that suggested there might be some risk in hiring her. That is, she answered yes to each of those questions. During the interview, you could ask her these two questions:

1. (pertaining to item A) "You mentioned on the survey that if someone is clever enough to take a large sum of money, he should be allowed to keep it. What are your thoughts on that situation?"
2. (pertaining to item B) "You indicated that sometimes it is justified to take money from an employer without permission. How did you come to that conclusion?"

Exhibit 4-11. Sample Candidate Rating Sheet for an applicant based on a character test.

	Risk Rating
Character Test	
▪ Drugs/drinking	↑
▪ Alienation from workplace/work ethic	→
▪ Trustworthiness	↑

Notes: ↑ = low risk; → = moderate risk; ↓ = high risk.

You can then listen to the applicant's responses to decide if the answers make sense or not. If her answers seem reasonable, you may want to consider her a viable candidate. However, if the applicant's rationale for each answer seems risky or even alarming, then it would be best to pass up that candidate and to find another one who earns low-risk or moderate-risk ratings and who explains answers in a manner you judge to be safe and trustworthy.

After testing for character, the final step is to fill in the Candidate Rating Sheet on each trait the test predicts. A typical candidate's Candidate Rating Sheet may look like the one shown in Exhibit 4-11. This candidate's scores yield a low risk on drugs and alcohol, a moderate risk on alienation from the workplace or work ethic, and a low risk on trustworthiness.

Notes

1. "One-Third Predict Increase in Usage," *Human Resource Executive,* November 15, 1992, p. 83.
2. Kenneth Pearlman, Frank L. Schmidt, and John E. Hunter, "Validity Generalization Results for Tests Used to Predict Job Proficiency and Training Success in Clerical Occupations," *Journal of Applied Psychology,* Vol. 65, No. 4 (Winter 1980): pp. 373–406.
3. Robert P. Tett, Douglas N. Jackson, and Mitchell Rothstein, "Personality Measures as Predictors of Job Performance: A Meta-Analytic Review," *Personnel Psychology* (Winter 1991), pp. 703 and 727.
4. Michael W. Mercer, *Behavior Forecaster™ Test* (Chicago: Mercer Systems, Inc., 1991).

5. Ibid.
6. James Q. Wilson, "Uncommon Sense About the IQ Debate," *Fortune,* January 11, 1993, p. 99.
7. Michael W. Mercer, *Abilities Forecaster™ Test* (Chicago: Mercer Systems, Inc., 1991).
8. Robert W. Cormack, *P.A.S.S.-III® D.A.T.A.® Survey* (Oak Brook, Ill.: Personnel Systems Corporation, 1987).

5

Tests for Predicting Applicants' Job Success

Part II: Technical Skills Tests, Work Simulations and Assessment Centers, and Evaluations of Executive Candidates

This chapter shows how to use three types of preemployment testing methods that often need to be customized. These testing or assessment methods are:

1. Technical skills tests
2. Work simulations and assessment center exercises
3. Evaluations of executive candidates

I also discuss legal guidelines for the use of testing methods.

Technical Skills Tests

A skills test predicts how well an applicant could do the sort of technical work required to succeed in a particular job. The most commonly used one is a typing test. Others include tests to evaluate candidates on their use of computer programs, equipment, or machinery. Many technical skills tests are hand-scored. However, they sometimes can be taken and scored on a computer.

Example of a Technical Skills Test

One technical skills test evaluates the job-related abilities of insurance claims processors.[1] It uses job-related situations and problems to measure how quickly and accurately applicants for an insurance claims processor position can handle or learn to do typical claims processing work.

This job-content valid instrument tests five skill dimensions: two typing dimensions and three thinking dimensions. These dimensions are:

- Typing skills
  —Speed on keyboard typing
  —Accuracy on keyboard typing
- Thinking skills
  —Comprehension
  —Calculation
  —Coding

The test mimics the environment in which the applicant would work. It does this with simplified computer screens and with the kind of forms and documents that claims processors are required to interpret and resolve.

The optimal candidate receives high scores on both typing and thinking. However, if there is no such candidate in the applicant pool, managers can at least clearly see who has the best potential for doing the job successfully. For example, someone with a high typing score but low thinking score may not do well on the job. Such a person would have difficulty figuring out what to do with claim form information. By contrast, someone with low or moderate typing scores but high thinking scores may be more trainable. If no better applicant materializes by the time the hiring must be done, then the company may decide to hire such a person, because typing skills can be learned much more readily than thinking skills.

Work Simulations and Assessment Center Exercises

The basic idea behind work simulations and assessment center exercises is to let those who make the hiring decisions watch and rate candidates as they use their job-related skills. This is quite different from listening to candidates during interviews or from examining test scores. There are, after all, some job-related abilities that can be better evaluated when they are seen in action than they can be evaluated in an interview or test.

For example, it would be absurd for a company to hire someone to do over-the-phone sales or other phone work without holding one or more phone conversations with each suitable applicant. Only in such phone discussions can the hiring manager actually hear how the person comes across and handles phone work.

Another example involves choosing candidates for team membership in a highly participative manufacturing department. Tests and interviews can pick up many teamwork-oriented attributes, but observing candidates interacting in a teamwork simulation also could yield valuable insights into their competence in participatively managed operations.

A more elaborate approach to using work simulations and other exercises is to develop a full-blown assessment center. The assessment center method originated during World War II when the Office of Strategic Services (OSS) evaluated candidates for intelligence work overseas. Later, in the mid-1950s, American Telephone and Telegraph began predicting management potential by using assessment centers.[2]

Since then, business organizations have adopted assessment center methods both for evaluating job candidates and for training and development programs for current employees. Given the time (often two days or longer), rather hefty cost, and fairly large number of people involved, however most assessment centers are used for employee training and development rather than for candidate selection.

Two assessment center experts, Douglas W. Bray and William C. Byham, explain how they work:

An assessment center is organized around a set of dimensions [or job-related criteria] matching the requirements of the target job. These dimensions, in turn, determine the exercises to be used. This is particularly germane to the behavioral [or work] simulations, which are designed to parallel the job without duplicating it. This latter restriction is to eliminate specific job knowledge, in which candidates might differ, so as to focus on generic job skills.[3]

Types of behavioral or work simulations used in assessment centers include the following:

- *Individual skill demonstrations.* For example, such an exhibition may include candidates:
  —Delivering presentations
  —Writing a memo, letter, or report
  —Editing written materials
- *Interaction simulations.* For example, job-related interactions may be between:
  —A boss and a subordinate
  —Two peers
  —A client service or salesperson and a customer
  Interaction simulations also may stage phone conversations on tasks such as telemarketing or customer service. Simulating such situations could form the basis of interaction exercises.
- *Group exercises.* For instance, a job may require a candidate to work predominantly in groups to analyze and resolve problems. Such group endeavors could be fabricated into an exercise in which each candidate participates.
- *In-basket exercises.* This simulates the kind of administrative work that comes across an employee's desk. For example, a candidate might be given an in-basket such as would ordinarily sit on her desk. The in-basket would contain materials the candidate must read, understand, and take action on. Some of the job-related actions an in-basket exercise might include are:

—Scheduling appointments

—Filling in a calendar

—Handling emergencies that arise

—Answering typical memos or letters

—Handling letters from grieving customers or managers

—Making recommendations on a report

—Reading and using pertinent magazine or newsletter articles to improve one's job performance

Using Work Simulations and Assessment Center Exercises

If you opt for work simulations and assessment center exercises, there are seven main steps to follow.[4]

1. *Plan which jobs are appropriate for using work simulations or assessment center exercises.* For instance, some jobs may lend themselves to simulations while others do not. Decide which jobs could benefit from having candidates go through work simulations or more detailed assessment center exercises.

2. *Do a job analysis.* Find out how people currently succeeding in a particular job actually do it. Also, take into account how the job will change. From this information, list the job-related criteria needed for job success.

3. *Select work simulations or exercises to use.* These simulations or exercises should tap into the extent to which a candidate meets the job-related criteria uncovered in Step 2. As described earlier, these activities may include individual skill demonstrations, interaction simulations, group exercises, and in-basket exercises.

4. *Train assessors or raters.* These people must be taught to:

—Instruct applicants in how to carry out the work simulations or exercises

—Observe and take notes on the job-related abilities and behaviors that will be rated

—Rate candidates on rating or evaluation forms

5. *Plan assessment facilities.* Decide where the simulations and exercises will take place and what special equipment, such

as flipcharts, transparency projectors, phones, or tables and chairs may be needed.

6. *Conduct work simulations or assessment center exercises.* This includes:

—Candidates doing the simulations or exercises
—Assessors observing and taking notes on specific behaviors that relate to each job criterion being assessed
—Assessors rating each candidate on the relevant job-related criteria

7. *Write assessment report on each candidate.* This includes:

—Notes on behaviors observed that relate to each criterion for the job
—Rating on each dimension
—Overall rating of candidate

Example of Work Simulation

Evaluating candidates on their "stand-up" presentation skills provides a good use of the work simulation method. Quite a few professional and managerial jobs require people to prepare and deliver impressive presentations, either when they are giving speeches or when they are conducting workshops. In fact, their presentation skills could make or break their performance on the job. While an interviewer could *ask* such candidates about their presentation skills, a more useful method would be to *observe* applicants actually delivering a presentation. Here's how to arrange such a work simulation:

1. Give the candidate some information about a hypothetical presentation she must deliver.
2. Supply the candidate with materials to make visual aids, such as flipcharts or transparencies.
3. Allow the candidate about an hour to prepare a presentation lasting up to fifteen minutes.
4. Have the assessors, armed with work simulation rating sheets, watch the candidate deliver her presentation.
5. Assessors then rate the candidate on the rating sheet.
6. Assessors compare behavioral observations and ratings

and come up with the final arrow ratings used on the Candidate Rating Form.

The *Presentation Simulation Rating Sheet* may look like that shown in Exhibit 5-1. A job analysis revealed that a presentation is most successful when it has the following characteristics:

- Is easy to understand
- Makes use of visual aids
- Shows a good presentation style
- Stays within the prescribed time limits

To help assessors, there is a list of behaviors to look for that appears after each criterion, along with room for assessors to write their observations of the candidate. Each assessor would give arrow ratings on each criterion as well as an overall rating.

The overall rating given by each assessor would go onto the Candidate Rating Sheet. For example, if candidate Terry Smith received an up arrow (↑) and Chris Jones earned a sideways arrow (→), the rating sheet would be filled in as shown in Exhibit 5-2.

Executive Evaluations

A top-notch executive provides an organization with what it needs to grow and prosper. By the same token, an executive who turns in a below-average performance can wreak havoc on a company's bottom line.

Given the critical importance of hiring top-notch executive talent, some companies ask an industrial psychologist to conduct special evaluations of executive candidates.[5] Such an evaluation goes beyond the assessments made by most interviews and tests in that it is thoroughly customized for the specific executive position under consideration. The evaluation also entails much conferring between the industrial psychologist and the company executive authorized to make this vital hiring decision. Given the importance of selecting excellent executives, these customized evaluations can prove to be worth more than

Exhibit 5-1.   Presentation Simulation Rating Sheet assessing candidates' skills in delivering speeches or conducting workshops.

Candidate's Name: _____   Date: _____
Assessor's Name: _____
Instructions:
> *During* the candidate's presentation, note particularly the specific behaviors that characterize the presenter with respect to the four categories assessed.
> *After* the candidate concludes, circle your rating of each behavior, then give an overall rating of the performance.
> Ratings are as follows: ↓ = poor; → = average; ↑ = good.

Categories and Behaviors to Observe	*Behavioral Rating*		
EASY TO UNDERSTAND			
_____ Well organized, uses outline.	↓	→	↑
Observations:			
_____ Clearly explains ideas.	↓	→	↑
Observations:			
_____ Uses clear and correct pronunciation.	↓	→	↑
Observations:			
_____ Uses layperson's terms.	↓	→	↑
Observations:			
_____ Does not overwhelm with statistics.	↓	→	↑
Observations:			
USE OF VISUAL AIDS			
_____ Uses visual aids, such as flipcharts or transparencies.	↓	→	↑
Observations:			
_____ Uses aids that are easy for entire audience to read or figure out.	↓	→	↑
Observations:			
_____ Uses aids that have an uncluttered appearance.	↓	→	↑
Observations:			
PRESENTATION STYLE			
_____ Does not read presentation.	↓	→	↑
Observations:			
_____ Maintains eye contact with audience.	↓	→	↑
Observations:			
_____ Speaks loudly enough for everyone to hear.	↓	→	↑

Observations:
_____ Talks with enthusiasm. ↓ → ↑
Observations:
_____ Avoids distracting body language or ↓ → ↑
      habits, such as playing with pens or
      pocket change.
Observations:
_____ Does not turn back to audience while ↓ → ↑
      talking.
Observations:
_____ Wears professional-looking clothing. ↓ → ↑
Observations:

TIMING

Time limit for presentation: _____ ↓ → ↑
      minutes.
Time candidate took: _____ minutes.

* * * * *

OVERALL RATING: ↓ → ↑

---

their weight in gold when they help a company hire the very best.

Doing Executive Evaluations

There are typically five steps in customized evaluations of candidates for executive positions:

1. *The executive to whom the candidate would report discusses the job with the industrial psychologist.* In this conversation, the executive delineates the job-related criteria the candidate must meet and the duties he or she would be responsible for.

2. *The industrial psychologist tests and interviews each candidate for the position.* This includes:

- In-depth testing of each candidate for one to four hours
- Interviewing each candidate for two to four hours
- Writing an extensive report on each candidate, including

Exhibit 5-2.   Candidate Rating Sheet on Terry Smith and Chris Jones.

	Terry Smith	*Chris Jones*
Interviewer #1	↑	↑
Interviewer #2	↑	↑
Behavior test	↑	↓
Mental abilities test	↑	↑
Work simulation (on presentation)	↑	→

predicting how well—or poorly—the candidate will do if hired for the executive position

3. *The industrial psychologist calls the executive making the hiring decision to discuss each candidate.*

4. *The executive making the hiring decision confers with the industrial psychologist before finally determining which candidate is most likely to succeed on the job.*

5. *After someone is hired, the industrial psychologist may meet with the just-hired executive to discuss recommendations for helping that person succeed.* These recommendations are based on the psychologist's in-depth executive evaluation of the candidate.

Example of an Executive Evaluation

A furniture company desired to hire a new vice-president of manufacturing and industrial engineering. It narrowed its list of candidates down to four, and I then evaluated each of these four finalists. My report on one of the candidates appears in Exhibit 5-3.

The report has two main sections:

1. Recommendations to management
2. Evaluation of the candidate, in terms of his/her:
   a. Motivations
   b. Problem-solving approach
   c. Communications skills
   d. Management style
   e. Interpersonal style
   f. Personality and temperament

(text continues on page 112)

Exhibit 5-3. Customized evaluation of executive candidate.

CANDIDATE: Mr. K   CANDIDATE FOR: Vice-President of Manufacturing and Industrial Engineering

RECOMMENDATIONS TO MANAGEMENT

Mr. K is an average candidate for the position of Vice-President of Manufacturing and Industrial Engineering at your company. He has assets in a number of areas. He also definitely needs to improve certain key skills.

Among Mr. K's strengths is his detail-focused, analytical, careful method of proceeding on practically everything he tackles. He invariably makes sure that every "i" is dotted and every "t" crossed. As such, your company could rest assured that all Mr. K's projects would be handled with an eye to perfection.

His most pronounced motivation is to achieve results. He is a hard-working, conscientious manager. His listening skills are fairly good. He also keeps his head up high by maintaining a basically positive attitude in all his endeavors.

Important with respect to your company's goals for this position, Mr. K works on projects in a comparatively consultative manner. He also shows a strong desire to train others in the concepts and technology that must be understood and implemented.

Despite many favorable attributes, Mr. K also shows some potential drawbacks that your company should take into account in deciding whether or not to hire him. One drawback is the flip side of one of Mr. K's strengths, namely, his extremely detail-focused mind-set. Specifically, Mr. K often gets bogged down in details. This causes him to take a long time to finish what he starts. He always finishes what he begins, but he takes longer than others to do so. Additionally, he can get quite wordy as he enters into more of the details than most people want or need to know.

His ability to "read" people could be better. Your company's Vice-President of Manufacturing and Industrial Engineering is required to interact with a lot of people. Thus, the ability to "read" others and then to use those insights would prove highly beneficial to the successful candidate. By not carefully "reading" people, Mr. K often misses cues as to how he strikes others.

Mr. K exhibits only a moderate amount of friendliness. Although he tries to come off friendly when he first meets someone, his initial smile seems forced rather than genuine. People notice such behavior. He also tends to overlook that he ought to relate to the person he is with *as a*

(continues)

Exhibit 5-3   *(continued)*

person—and not just as one technical, precise mind communicating with another technical, precise mind.

After your staff members got to know Mr. K, they probably would accustom themselves to his interpersonal style. Until then, these weaknesses could make for some rocky times during the critical period when he is trying to establish smooth working relationships.

Mr. K's weaknesses could be overcome to a degree through specific training and development experiences. If your company looks favorably on his candidacy, then these actions would help enhance his job performance:

1. *Provide Mr. K with interpersonal skills training.* This training should include fundamentals, such as how to start and continue a friendly conversation. It should also emphasize techniques on how to "read" other people and build rapport.
2. *Set time limits on his projects.* Mr. K gets so wrapped up in small details that he takes longer to complete assignments than many other people do. Therefore, management should monitor how fast he completes projects. He always finishes what he starts, but his relative slowness could affect the scheduling of important projects.
3. *Send him to negotiation skills training.* Mr. K is quite precise and organized. He expects others to be the same. However, in the real world, very few people are as precise and organized as Mr. K. His ultrahigh expectations in this regard could cause problems with colleagues and subordinates. Training and coaching on how to persuade, influence, and negotiate would help him learn how to handle such inevitable interpersonal roadblocks to his on-the-job effectiveness.

EVALUATION OF THE CANDIDATE

MOTIVATIONS

Mr. K is strongly motivated to achieve his goals. He feels extremely dedicated to completing tasks assigned him or that he sets himself.

He loves to be busy and involved and thrives on maintaining a very high level of activity. As such, he enjoys diving into hundreds of small details and then figuring out what to do with them.

He is a take-charge sort of individual. He enjoys assuming a leadership role and making sure that projects get carried out.

PROBLEM-SOLVING APPROACH

He analyzes problems in a very slow, extraordinarily cautious and methodical manner. Mr. K takes a good deal more time than most people do when it comes to problem solving. This fact stems from Mr. K's very detail-focused nature. As an astoundingly analytical person, Mr. K digs into multitudes of tiny details to diagnose situations. This takes a good deal of time.

Using these same skills, Mr. K plans quite carefully. He lays out the steps and timetables needed to complete the projects on hand. He makes sure that every detail is tended to before he proceeds to his next venture.

COMMUNICATIONS SKILLS

Mr. K expresses his thoughts in an easy-to-understand manner. People know exactly what he is trying to say. He clearly communicates both technical details and concepts.

However, because he is an extremely detail-focused person, Mr. K's speaking style can become pedantic in that he often overemphasizes minutiae that his listeners do not need or want to hear. He does not seem to realize how very wordy he sounds.

He listens pretty well. When people request information or ideas from Mr. K, he gives them exactly what they want. He also checks with people to make sure that they have understood what he said.

Mr. K thinks quite a lot before he puts pen to paper. He makes sure that he writes down all the information required to express what he wants. He sometimes overlooks a few grammatical rules, however, and that detracts slightly from the quality of his writing.

MANAGEMENT STYLE

Mr. K's management style is marked by how thoroughly organized, exacting, and precise he is. As such, any project he manages will be distinguished by the thoughtful attention given to each and every step.

He works in a fairly collaborative manner. Mr. K puts emphasis on jointly planning projects he undertakes with others. To do so, he uses a consultative approach to managing. This is how Mr. K transfers his knowledge and expertise to others.

Mr. K views part of his management role as that of a trainer. He uses training as a means of developing people. Training others also helps him to bring about the adoption of new methods and technologies that he thinks would produce improved results.

(continues)

Exhibit 5-3   *(continued)*

INTERPERSONAL STYLE

Mr. K works hard to convey a friendly impression when he first meets someone. After this initial stab at friendliness, however, Mr. K lapses into a more technically oriented—and less people-oriented—focus. While doing so, Mr. K is very serious and he certainly comes across as "all business."

He displays limited ability or desire to "read" other people's personalities. Mr. K tends to take others' behavior at face value. As he does this, Mr. K comes across as rather emotionally aloof. He is not actually cold-hearted, but normally he is not a warm person with whom to interact.

PERSONALITY AND TEMPERAMENT

Mr. K is a rather uncomplicated fellow. Basically, he keeps himself organized, and he handles most situations in a straightforward manner. Mr. K also displays an above-average energy level.

Intrinsically, he displays a positive attitude. Despite a number of career setbacks, Mr. K picks himself up, brushes himself off, and figures out how to proceed toward his goals. Such persistence and dogged determination are evident in every activity he tackles.

THIS EVALUATION OF THE CANDIDATE WAS PREPARED BY:
Michael W. Mercer, Ph.D.
Industrial Psychologist

The next step after doing executive evaluations is to fill in the Candidate Rating Sheet with final ratings on each candidate based on the executive evaluation, interviews, reference checks, and any other useful information. For example, since the executive candidate evaluated in Exhibit 5-3 earned an average rating in the evaluation, he would receive a sideways-pointing arrow.

Legal Guidelines for Testing

The legal guidelines for using tests are the same as for all other applicant evaluation methods, including interviews and reference checks.[6] Specifically, any applicant screening procedure should be:

- Job-related
- Valid
- Reliable
- Used by the company in a nondiscriminatory manner

Only tests that are job-related should be used to assess job applicants. In other words, an employer should not be satisfied with just any preemployment test or questionnaire. Instead, the employer must first pinpoint the specific knowledge, skills or abilities, and personality characteristics needed by an employee to succeed in a particular job and then look for tests that measure those specific attributes.

In fact, as would be expected, research shows that preemployment personality or behavior testing results have higher predictive validity when a company first does a job analysis to pinpoint the job-related criteria needed to succeed on a specific job and then chooses a test or tests to measure those specific job-related criteria.[7]

Interestingly, a classic study of the validity of a wide array of selection procedures revealed that mental abilities tests have the highest predictive validity correlation.[8] This means that of all the candidate screening procedures, mental ability tests prove most accurate at predicting actual on-the-job success.

Because of the way that tests are developed, a test must first be reliable before it can be valid. As such, valid tests are, by research techniques and definition, also reliable tests.

All thoroughly developed tests a company might consider using should have a technical manual. This manual describes the research used to establish the test's reliability and validity. A manager interested in using a particular test can ask to see the technical manual. Such manuals often delve into the research methods used and the statistical results they yielded. This makes them hard to understand for people who are not trained in research and statistics. In this case, the manager choosing the tests should feel free to ask the industrial psychologist or other professional who developed them any questions about the technical manual's contents that seem hard to grasp.

The main points to look for in a test's technical manual are (1) whether the research used in developing the test was in-depth, and (2) whether the test's validity *and* reliability are "statistically significant." The statistical significance of research results is indicated by $p <$ probability values or levels of significance. In general, the statistics summarizing the test's validity and reliability should show that the $p <$ values for validity and reliability are $p < .05$ or, if the number after $p <$ is not .05, then that number should be lower to indicate even better statistical significance, for example, $p < .01$ or $p < .001$. By looking for such validity and reliability statistics, the test buyer can see if the test has research-based, statistically significant validity and reliability.

A well-done technical research manual can make a company's testing easier to defend in court than interviewing as a candidate evaluation technique. For instance, Edward B. Mitchell, a labor and employment lawyer with the law firm of Thompson, Hine and Flory in Cincinnati, writes:

> For the most part, employers using commercially available standardized paper-and-pencil tests will be able to demonstrate the validity of such tests where required through the use of validity studies which have been conducted by the company which markets the test. For that reason, the use of standardized paper-and-pencil tests which have wide application to success on many types of jobs and which have been the subject of extensive validation studies through the course of their use have a distinct advantage to an employer. Subjective selection criteria, such as the impressions a supervisor formed during a thirty-minute interview, are far more difficult to defend. If procedures such as interviews result in disparate impact requiring validation, the employer is effectively dead in the water since there is virtually no way for any but the largest employers to statistically validate those subjective determinations. If the procedure cannot be validated, under [equal employment opportunity] guidelines the disparate impact of the procedure is enough to establish unlawful discrimination.[9]

"Disparate impact," as mentioned in this statement, is a legal term referring to a type of hiring-related discrimination in which an employment practice or procedure (such as a test or interview) results in discrimination against a protected class. Such a practice is unlawful unless the employer can prove that the practice is job-related or a business necessity. In practice, disparate impact is considered to exist when the hiring rate for any racial, ethnic, or gender group is less than 80 percent of the rate for the highest selection rate. Thus, if a company can prove that it makes *valid* predictions as to how well each candidate will perform on the job (and bases its hiring decision on this factor), then it has a basis on which to defend itself in the eventuality of charges of discrimination being brought against it.[10]

Because most companies do no research on the validity of the interviews they conduct, they essentially possess no defense for basing their hiring decisions on interviews alone. By contrast, tests must be validated and, as such, provide companies with a basis for showing that their predictions of job-related performance are valid and reliable.[11]

Finally, legally defensible testing should be used in a nondiscriminatory manner. This means that a company can have a test that fulfills the first three criteria of a legally suitable test (that is, the test is job-related, valid, and reliable), yet if it uses the test to discriminate, then the company (*not* the test) may be legally at fault.

For example, I was once asked by the president of a manufacturing company to help that company to begin using tests in a nondiscriminatory manner in the hiring of factory workers. He then proceeded to show me a magnificently developed, thoroughly researched test that was job-related, valid, and reliable. In fact, the test was developed by an industrial psychologist with a very fine reputation. I told the company president that the test met essential standards. So, why did the company need my testing expertise?

The president told me that the company had been involved in a four-year lawsuit because it had used the job-related, valid, reliable test to hire *only* people of certain groups. The company purposely did *not* hire people from certain minority groups. In fact, it never seriously considered candidates from those minority groups. It was using the test in a discriminatory manner. This practice led the company into a huge, expensive, time-consuming heap of legal and financial trouble.

Misconceptions About the Legalities of Testing

It is amazing how many managers are uninformed about the legal aspects of using preemployment tests. Based on my own informal survey, it would seem that many managers misinterpret how tests have been perceived in highly publicized court cases.

Probably the biggest case involving testing was *Griggs v. Duke Power Company* in 1971.[12] In this case, a utility company gave candidates for a janitorial job an intelligence test. Few blacks met the standards set by the company, and few blacks were hired.

Many people misinterpret the court's decision in this case, which found against the power company, as a blow against testing. The four legal criteria for screening procedures reveal that the test itself was *not* illegal, and the court in fact never said that the test was unlawful. All the data on the test used by the utility company show that the test exhibited high validity and reliability—two of the four key elements of any legally defensible selection technique.

However, Duke Power Company appeared not to have taken into account the two other criteria of a useful and legally justifiable applicant screening procedure. Specifically, the company could not show that the valid, reliable intelligence test it used was either job-related or used by the company in a nondiscriminatory manner.

Another widely publicized, yet often misunderstood case, was *Soroka v. Dayton Hudson Corp.*[13] In this case, a retail store company gave a seemingly *non*job-related test to security guard candidates. The test chosen was in fact a test developed to assess patients for mental illness—in other words, a test not originally intended for workplace testing.

The test is a well-validated and reliable one for detecting mental disorders, such as neurosis, psychosis, hypochondria, and antisocial behavior. It can be argued that the test might uncover some useful data about candidates for a security guard position. For instance, it probably would be useful to know whether a security guard is likely to act impulsively or to exhibit antisocial behavior.

However, the test was deemed too clinical and not sufficiently job-related. It contained questions that, while useful in uncovering mental illnesses, are inappropriate to ask of candidates for an ordinary job. For example, the test asked questions about applicants' sexual behavior, questions that are highly inappropriate—in fact, taboo—in the workplace.

Nevertheless, some people misinterpret this case as an attack on testing. Such a conclusion is totally false. There is nothing in the court documents to the effect that testing per se is illegal. The company's fault lay in not making sure that it used a test that was thoroughly *job-related* and valid for *workplace* testing of job candidates.

Soroka v. Dayton Hudson Corp. illustrates the importance of using only those tests that have been (1) developed and researched specifically for workplace testing and (2) whose validity and reliability for workplace testing have been established.

Problems concerning these two factors arise because most tests are not developed for workplace testing. They are developed by *clinical* (mental health) psychologists to assess mental disorders.

By contrast, tests meant for workplace testing are generally developed by *industrial* psychologists to evaluate job candidates. Therefore, managers considering tests should inquire if the test's research and purpose focus on workplace testing, *not* on mental health testing. This distinction becomes even more crucial as companies increasingly pay attention to hiring people because they can perform job-related duties regardless of their physical or mental disabilities.

Exhibit 5-4 condenses the main steps involved in using tests to predict candidates' on-the-job performance.

Exhibit 5-4.   Summary checklist on how to test job applicants.

_____ Do a job analysis to determine the job-related attributes needed to succeed on the job.

_____ Choose or develop validated tests that predict job-related criteria. These tests may include any or all of the following:
—Behavior tests
—Mental abilities tests
—Character tests
—Work simulations or assessment center exercises
—Technical skills tests
—Evaluations of executive candidates

_____ Pinpoint test scores that a potentially successful applicant would get on the test. As appropriate, use the following methods:
—Concurrent validity study
—Predictive validity study
—National norms
—Armchairing or Delphi Method

_____ Administer the test(s) to candidates for the job.

_____ Compare each candidate's scores with the scores a potentially successful applicant would get on the test.

_____ Fill in Candidate Rating Sheet.

Notes

1. *Claims Processing Proficiency Assessment* (New York: Q Technologies, 1991).
2. A. Howard and D. W. Bray, *Managerial Lives in Transition: Advancing Age and Changing Times* (New York: Guilford Press, 1988); G. C. Thornton, III and W. C. Byham, *Assessment Centers and Managerial Performance* (New York: Academic Press, 1982).
3. Douglas W. Bray and William C. Byham, "Assessment Centers and Their Derivatives," *Journal of Continuing Higher Education,* Winter 1991, p. 8.
4. William C. Byham. Personal conversation with author, December 22, 1992.
5. Michael W. Mercer, *Turning Your Human Resources Department Into a Profit Center* (New York: AMACOM, 1989), pp. 202–207.
6. J. D. Thorne and Michael W. Mercer, "Legal Rules and Bottom Line Reasons for Pre-Employment Testing," *Die Casting Engineer,* March/April, 1993, pp. 50–51.
7. Robert P. Tett, Douglas N. Jackson, and Mitchell Rothstein, "Personality Measures as Predictors of Job Performance: A Meta-Analytic Review," *Personnel Psychology,* Winter 1991, pp. 703 and 727.
8. John E. Hunter and Ronda F. Hunter, "Validity and Utility of Alternative Predictors of Job Performance," *Psychological Bulletin,* Vol. 96, No. 1, 1984, p. 90.

9. Edward B. Mitchell, *To Test or Not to Test: Legal Considerations in Employment Testing* (Cincinnati: Thompson, Hine and Flory, January 1992), p. 3.
10. William R. Tracey, *The Human Resources Glossary: A Complete Desk Reference for HR Professionals* (New York: AMACOM, 1991), p. 97. Adapted by permission of the publisher. © 1991 AMACOM, a division of American Management Association, New York. All rights reserved.
11. J. D. Thorne and Michael W. Mercer, "Legal Rules and Bottom Line Reasons for Pre-Employment Testing."
12. *Griggs v. Duke Power Company,* 401 U.S. 424, 1971.
13. *Soroka v. Dayton Hudson Corporation,* 238 Cal. App. 3rd 654 (1991).

6

Reference Checks to Forecast Candidates' Performance

A reference check typically consists of contacting a candidate's previous employers so that you can inquire about the applicant's on-the-job performance. While this sounds simple in theory, it proves tough in practice. What is making it harder to obtain accurate reports on candidates' past job performance is employers' mounting fear of getting sued by an ex-employee.

Martha H. Peak of the American Management Association sums up the predicament in this way:

> At most companies today, corporate policy prohibits managers from giving references for former employees. Yet these same companies *require* references before a job offer can be made.
>
> Recent—and extremely expensive—defamation suits have made employers understandably gun-shy about reference requests. For this reason, the word is coming down . . . : All requests for references should be directed to the human resources department. There, trained HR managers usually will politely verify the applicant's name, job title and dates of employment—nothing else.[1]

Given this problem, what are you to do? In the past, a manager could round up some good job candidates, call up their former bosses, and find out straight from the horse's mouth how wonderfully or poorly (or in between) each one did on the job. Today such easy reference checks are probably a thing of the past.

Fortunately, there are two ways of doing reference checks that can yield accurate and useful information. These methods include:

- Getting ex-employers to open up and reveal useful information about former employees
- Doing background checks of verifiable data on candidates

Getting Accurate Reference Checks

To do a meaningful reference check follow these four steps:

Step 1: List the job-related criteria you will be checking up on. This should prove easy because you have already developed a list of job-related criteria for use in the candidate interview. For example, Exhibit 2-7 illustrates an Interview Guide Form, including job-related criteria, for a sales job at a particular company. Just make a few small adjustments in this same Interview Guide Form to transform it into a Reference Checking Form suitable for taking notes on during your reference check phone calls. Exhibit 6-1 shows how it will look.

Step 2: Collect information on the Reference Checking Form. You do this by two means:
1. Making phone calls to the candidate's ex-employers
2. Gathering verifiable background data on the candidate
There are at least five ways of getting over-the-phone reference check information that won't leave you in the dark. These methods are used by managers who have discovered ways to gather useful information despite roadblocks. Given the increasing difficulty of getting useful information from former employers, managers who want to hire the best may need to use all five methods to amass the facts most crucial to making a decision.

First, *directly ask the candidate's ex-bosses for information.* Just call the ex-bosses at work and talk with them. Although more

(text continues on page 124)

Exhibit 6-1. Reference Checking Form for sales job applicant.

REFERENCE CHECKING FORM
for CANDIDATE FOR *SALESPERSON*

CANDIDATE'S NAME: _____

REFERENCE CHECKER'S NAME: _____

PERSON CALLED TO SERVE AS REFERENCE ON

CANDIDATE:

      Name: _____

      Title: _____

  Organization: _____

 Phone Number: _____

  Date Called: _____

BASIC REFERENCE CHECK: Did this person verify the candidate's:

- Job title(s)   Yes   No
- Dates of employment   Yes   No

Job-Related Criterion	*Notes*
Assertiveness	Notes:

_____ Took charge of projects or
       tasks.

_____ Did not back off.

_____ Expressed opinions
       firmly.

_____ Let people know his/her
       viewpoints.

                                 Rating: ↓ → ↑

Prefers Working Solo   Notes:

_____ Enjoyed working alone.

_____ Was most productive
       when working alone.

                                 Rating: ↓ → ↑

Persuasiveness   Notes:

_____ Swayed others' opinions
       and actions.

_____ Influenced others of di-
       verse interpersonal
       styles.

                                 Rating: ↓ → ↑

Handles Obstacles Well   Notes:

_____ Bounced back, showed re-
       silience.

_____ Was emotionally ob-
       jective.

_____ Viewed problems as op-
     portunities in disguise.
_____ Overcame roadblocks.

Rating: ↓ → ↑

Optimism	Notes:

_____ Focused on solutions, not
     problems.
_____ Focused on opportunities,
     not drawbacks.
_____ Had a "Can-Do" attitude.
_____ Did not mention burn-
     out or difficulty hand-
     ling high stress.

Rating: ↓ → ↑

High Energy	Notes:

_____ Was tireless.
_____ Had great stamina.
_____ Liked being very busy.
_____ Showed high energy.

Rating: ↓ → ↑

Being a Self-Starter	Notes:

_____ Completed tasks without
     being prodded.
_____ Disliked being told what
     to do.

Rating: ↓ → ↑

Desire for High Earnings	Notes:

_____ Considered money
     crucial.
_____ Discussed financial
     achievements and/or
     goals.
_____ Was enthusiastic about
     earning incentive pay.
_____ Desired pay linked to re-
     sults.

Rating: ↓ → ↑

OVERALL RATING OF THIS CANDIDATE: ↓ → ↑
(rating made by reference checker, not by candidate's
ex-boss or person providing reference)

and more managers have been warned not to divulge information about past employees, some are still willing to do so. A
friendly, collegial phone technique helps create the atmosphere
in which the ex-boss may feel inclined to disclose the kinds of
things you want to know.

Second, since many ex-bosses try to avoid giving complete
references, especially while they're at the office, *call the candidate's ex-boss at home.* Do this in the evening during the week or
over weekends. When the ex-boss answers, say, "[Candidate A]
applied for a job to work for me. He suggested I contact you for
a *personal* reference. That's why I'm calling you at home." Calling
this "a *personal* reference" makes it sound a bit less ominous
than calling it a business reference. Also, calling at home when
the ex-boss is away from work and likely to be more relaxed
makes this phone call seem out of the ordinary and more "personal" than a call to the office would seem.

Third, *call one of your friends or acquaintances at the candidate's
former employer,* if you know anyone who works there. Ask this
person to tell you about the candidate, *if* he or she is familiar
with the candidate's job performance. Or, ask the friend to provide you with an introduction to the candidate's ex-boss. This
method may work better than directly calling the candidate's
previous supervisor.

Fourth, if the candidate worked evening or night shifts,
then do not call during the day. Instead, *call the candidate's former
evening or night shift supervisors.* Companies often tell their day
shift managers not to give out detailed references on past employees. But because few people call the evening or night shift
supervisors to get references, these supervisors are often un-
aware that the company would prefer them not to talk about
ex-employees. Also, they may like the attention and feeling of
importance that being asked to give a reference provides. As
such, evening and night shift supervisors sometimes prove to be
great sources of information about applicants.

Fifth, if the candidate has held management positions, *call
the candidate's previous secretaries.* Preferably, call them at home,
where no co-workers are around to overhear or censor their remarks. As with any reference, use your judgment in gauging
how valid the information appears to be.

In addition to the five ways to make phone calls to the candidate's ex-employers, you also can gather verifiable background data on the candidate. This information may delve into items that could help determine an applicant's suitability for a particular job. Types of verifiable background data are the applicant's:

- Previous employment
- Criminal record (if any)
- Credit history
- Motor vehicle report
- Academic history
- Workers compensation claims

Such reference checks are discussed in more detail in the section of this chapter on "Legal Guidelines for Reference Checking."

Step 3: Rate the Candidate on the Reference Checking Form. This rating will reflect your own judgment as the reference checker, not the "ratings" given by the candidate's ex-bosses or other persons providing reference information.

Step 4: Put the overall reference check rating on the Candidate Rating Sheet by inserting the arrow rating for the candidate based on the information you gathered. Your Candidate Rating Sheet may look like the sheet prepared for applicants Terry Smith and Chris Jones shown in Exhibit 6-2.

Legal Guidelines for Reference Checking

Questions: What's all the commotion about? Why are organizations so terrified of discussing their former employees?

Answer: Organizations tremble at the possibility of ex-employees slapping them with lawsuits on two main grounds: (1) defamation and (2) invasion of privacy.[2]

In the first type of case, the company fears that something negative it says about an ex-worker may be considered defamatory. So, companies work hard to avoid making disparaging remarks about past employees, even when the employee's performance warrants a bad review.

Second, companies are scared of getting sued for invasion

Exhibit 6-2.   Candidate Rating Sheet on Terry Smith and Chris Jones.

	Candidates	
	Terry Smith	Chris Jones
Interviewer #1	↑	↑
Interviewer #2	↑	↑
Behavior test	↑	↓
Mental abilities test	↑	↑
Work simulation (presentation)	↑	→
Reference check	↑	→

of privacy. If the company reveals nonjob-related information or other information an ex-employee deems irrelevant—such as personal quirks that do not affect job performance—then the ex-employee may sue on grounds that his or her privacy has been violated.

Nevertheless, accurate reference checks can be beneficial in helping employers to avoid lawsuits brought on the charges of negligent hiring or termination or wrongful discharge.

Negligent hiring suits arise when (1) a company's employee commits a crime against someone while working on the premises and (2) the employer is held liable for not having uncovered the potential danger before placing the employee in the job. For instance, if a worker physically assaults a customer *and* the worker's history includes assault convictions, the company could be held liable for negligent hiring. This makes it very much in the interests of organizations to avoid making negligent hiring blunders.

A second legal reason for the importance of thorough reference checks is that they reduce the possibility of a company's hiring a below-average employee who later has to be terminated. After all, there are over six times more discharge-related lawsuits than there are hiring-related lawsuits.[3] This means that a company is much more likely to get sued for terminating an employee (even a below-average employee) than for not hiring the person in the first place.

With all these problems potentially popping up, what legal

points should an employer keep in mind when doing reference checks? It boils down to following the four basic principles of legally acceptable employment practices. Specifically, reference checks should be:

- Job-related
- Valid
- Reliable
- Used by the company in a nondiscriminatory manner

Let's talk first about these four points in relation to the typical over-the-phone reference checks most companies do. After that we can turn to background verification types of reference checks.

Obtaining *job-related* reference checks over the phone means that the company should seek only such information as is relevant to the criteria essential for doing the job successfully. Nonjob-related information should not be sought. For instance, it would be fine to call an applicant's former boss and ask if the applicant (1) showed up on time for work and (2) worked productively. These are two job-related concerns. However, it would *not* be job-related to ask about the applicant's home life or nonwork habits, despite the fact that such nonjob-related matters could affect whether the candidate showed up on time or accomplished his or her work goals.

Second, reference checks should be *valid*. This means that they should provide accurate information about the candidate. A problem affecting validity is caused when managers receive directives to make only positive remarks (or to say nothing at all) about former subordinates. Thus, the typical over-the-phone reference check may not yield valid information.

For example, the president (who also was a large shareholder) of a manufacturing company sought to hire a new chief financial officer (CFO). She found a seemingly good candidate in a man who used to work for a bank. The manufacturing company's president called this bank's president and asked about the candidate. The bank president made glowing remarks about the applicant. Given the enthusiastic reference and the manufacturing company president's good impression of the candidate in the interview (*no* testing was done on the candidate), she hired the man.

About a year later, the CFO embezzled money from the manufacturing company. When the president called the bank president to tell him about the embezzlement, he said to her, "Oh, he did the same thing here at the bank."

The company president, in a state of shock, asked the bank president, "Why didn't you tell me?"

The bank president replied, "Why should I? If I had, I could have been sued."

This of course is an extreme example, but many other organizations also experience trouble obtaining valid or accurate information from reference checks. For instance, a chain of upscale retail stores found that its reference checks were essentially worthless. When it hired salespeople, it would call candidates' former employers. However, it seldom learned the full story about the candidate. Unfortunately, not only did the reference checks possess low validity but most of the chain's store managers also made invalid or inaccurate predictions on the basis of their interviews of applicants. To overcome these problems, this company started using preemployment tests to get valid, objective predictions of how well each sales applicant would perform on the job.

All these validity problems point to the need for the reference checker to use judgment in deciding if the people providing the reference information are giving accurate or valid details. While such opinions are not scientific, they are often all the reference checker has to go on in gauging the validity or nonvalidity of information about candidates.

On top of the validity problem with reference checks is an often-occurring *reliability* problem. A reliable reference check yields information about an applicant that is repeated by at least two sources. For instance, if one reference says that a candidate did an outstanding job, with luck another reference will confirm that observation. That would give an aura of reliability to the information. Unfortunately, details uncovered in one call may not be repeated elsewhere. This lowers the reliability or dependability of data uncovered in typical over-the-phone reference checks.

Finally, the reference checks should be *used by the company in a nondiscriminatory manner.* This ought to be easy enough to do. Just use the *same* reference checking procedures for *all* candidates. Doing so decreases the chance of treating applicants from one group differently from the way you treat candidates from other groups. It is also good business practice to use consistent procedures in evaluating each candidate.

While over-the-phone types of reference checks are the most widely used, some organizations also check verifiable background data on applicants. These data concern the following[4]:

- Previous employment
- Criminal record, if any
- Credit history
- Motor vehicle report
- Academic history
- Workers compensation claims

Why are such checks necessary? To begin with, about a third of all résumés include false information.[5] So, verifying previous employment and academic history are the least any company should do.

There are other reasons for flushing out verifiable background information. For instance, a company hiring a driver would be wise to investigate the applicant's motor vehicle reports. Such reports may reveal crucial information—such as drunk driving or reckless driving convictions—that would negate an applicant's potential to do the job. Likewise, an organization hiring a security guard has good reason for wanting to know each candidate's criminal history to see if there is cause for alarm.

Previous employment history and academic history are easy to check. All you have to do is phone the former employers and schools listed by the candidate. Motor vehicle and criminal records, by contrast, have to be checked in all fifty states. This would be quite time-consuming for a company to do on its own. Fortunately, there are background reference checking services that handle these complicated multistate investigations. While the costs of such services may seem high, they are vastly lower than the cost of defending even one negligent hiring or termination lawsuit resulting from hiring a troublemaker or below-average person.

Despite these benefits, it is still important to look at how the four key legal principles relate to verifiable background checks. First, background checks should only look into *job-related* information. For instance, if the applicant is not going to drive as part of the job, then do not bother to check motor vehicle records. If, on the other hand, the job requires driving, then it is definitely job-related to look into the applicant's driving records.

Next, the information should be *valid* and *reliable*. Unless some big goof-up has occurred in the records investigated, the details gleaned from verifiable background checks should be accurate (valid) and dependable (reliable). Finally, these background checks should be done in a *nondiscriminatory manner*. As usual, do the checks on *all* potentially suitable candidates for the same job and not just on candidates who belong to certain groups.

Notes

1. Martha H. Peak, "Rumors, Lies and Innuendo," *Personnel*, December 1990, p. 12. Reprinted by permission of the publisher, from *Personnel*, December 1990. © 1990, American Management Association, New York. All rights reserved.
2. Kenneth L. Sovereign, *Personnel Law*, 2nd ed. (Englewood Cliffs, N.J.: Prentice-Hall, 1989), Chapter 9; and "Pitfalls of Withholding Reference Information," *Personnel Journal*, March 1990, p. 122.
3. John J. Donohue III and Peter Siegelman, "The Changing Nature of Employment Discrimination Litigation," *Stanford Law Review*, May 1991, p. 1016.
4. Michael W. Mercer, *Turning Your Human Resources Department Into a Profit Center* (New York: AMACOM, 1989), p. 210.
5. Carol Kleiman, "Fudging Credentials Now Much Riskier," *Chicago Tribune*, September 27, 1987, Section 8, p. 1.

7

Profit Improvement When You Hire the Best

How to Measure Your Hiring Successes in Dollars and Cents

The ultimate goal of hiring top-notch employees is, of course, to improve productivity and profits. Managers usually know in their hearts when an employee is helping measurably to improve the bottom line. They also know when a below-average or troublemaking employee is dragging down work effectiveness and morale or having a negative effect on countless other make-it-or-break-it workplace factors. Also, there are other nonfinancial, qualitative ingredients that come into play when a company hires the best—and avoids the rest.

Given how important these matters are, I will discuss in this chapter:

- An easy-to-use six-step method of calculating the cost-benefit ratio when companies hire the best
- Nonfinancial rewards managers reap when they hire top-notch employees
- Believe-it-or-not benefits accruing to validly evaluated candidates when they are *rejected* for a job

How to Measure Profit Improvement When You Hire the Best

A six-step profit improvement model is very useful for measuring the cost-benefits or return-on-investment of hiring high-quality employees. This six-step model is described and illustrated in detail in my book, *Turning Your Human Resources Department Into a Profit Center.*[1] The six steps appear in Exhibit 7-1.

Step 1, the *selection problem or opportunity,* involves simply listing the selection situations that could be improved by hiring the best. These problems or opportunities typically center on two *measurable* factors: productivity and turnover.

Step 2, the *cost of the selection problem,* involves listing all the costs resulting from a selection problem and then adding them up to arrive at the total cost. For instance, the costs may stem from low productivity or higher-than-desired turnover.

Of course, if the situation described in Step 1 is an opportunity rather than a problem, then there is no applicable *cost of the selection problem,* and this second step can be left blank. For example, a company may have productive salespeople but decide to work on hiring even more productive salespeople. Since this company's sales force is already doing well, there is no problem. Instead, the company can seize an opportunity to hire salespeople who are likely to be even more highly productive on the job.

Step 3, the *solution to the selection problem,* entails candidate evaluation techniques explained in this book. These techniques include interviews, tests, and reference checks.

Step 4, the *cost of solution,* or *cost of the selection method,* entails adding up the various costs of each selection method used. For instance, interviewing costs may include the interviewers' salaries and benefits and, if needed, the costs of training managers in how to interview. Tests used would cost money. Reference check costs could include the salary and benefits of the person doing the over-the-phone reference checks and/or the expenses of having a background checking service do the work.

Step 5 is the *$ improvement benefit*. This is calculated half a year to two years after the solution is implemented. It quantifies

Exhibit 7-1. Six-step model for measuring cost-benefits or return-on-investment when a company hires the best.

Step 1: Selection problem or opportunity
Step 2: Cost of selection problem
Step 3: Solution to selection problem or opportunity
Step 4: Cost of solution on selection method
Step 5: $ improvement benefit
Step 6: Cost-benefit ratio

Source: Michael W. Mercer, *Turning Your Human Resources Department Into a Profit Center* (New York: AMACOM, 1989).

the (1) decrease in costs from those noted in Step 2, the *cost of the selection problem,* or (2) increase in productivity or profits.

Finally, Step 6, the *cost-benefit ratio,* involves the ratio of Step 5, the *$ improvement benefit,* to Step 4, the *cost of solution.* For example, if the *$ improvement benefit* is $100,000 and the *cost of solution* is $5,000, then the *cost-benefit ratio* is 20:1. It should be noted that although the commonly used term is cost-benefit ratio, the resulting ratio actually gives the benefit before the cost.

Putting the Profit Improvement Model to Work

The following two examples showing how to put the Six-Step Profit Improvement Model into action examine:

1. Hiring salespeople who sell more
2. Reducing costly turnover and improving productivity

Hiring Salespeople Who Sell More

An office products company's sales force was essentially doing a good job. Its sales increased continually, and it seldom proved necessary to terminate any salesperson. However, the company's vice-president of sales and its president both noticed that some of their salespeople sold a great deal more than their colleagues did. It dawned on them that if they could hire more salespeople with behaviors and mental abilities akin to those of their high achievers, then (1) the sales force would be more productive, that is, sell more; and (2) the company would make bigger profits. The resulting Six-Step Profit Improvement Model outlining how they handled this opportunity appears as Exhibit 7-2.

To tackle the situation, the company asked me, as an industrial psychologist, to conduct a concurrent validity study. In this study, I tested the sales force using two tests, one predicting behavior on the job and the other forecasting candidates' job-related mental abilities.[2]

This study yielded the success pattern or profile of scores attained by the company's most productive salespeople. Then the two tests were used in evaluating all sales candidates. Before the tests came into use, interviews and reference checks alone were employed. Only candidates who got all up arrows on their tests, interviews, and reference checks (that is, predictions that they would do well on the job) were hired for the sales jobs. The *cost of solution,* or the cost of conducting the concurrent validity study and using the two tests for one year, was $4,000.

The resulting *$ improvement benefit* was $900,000 per year. This was calculated on the basis of a suggestion by the company's vice-president of sales. Specifically, he figured out the average annual sales made by the twenty salespeople he had hired *before* using testing in their first year of working for the company; this was $210,000 per year. Then, one year after hiring each new salesperson on the basis of the tests, he computed the new salespeople's average annual sales, which turned out to be $255,000 a year. In other words, the twenty original salespeople (hired without the tests) sold a total of $4,200,000 a year in their first year working for the company. By contrast, the twenty new salespeople (hired with the tests) tallied up $5,100,000 a year in their first year as salespeople for this company. The difference between these two totals yields the $900,000 a year *$ improvement benefit.*

Finally, the *cost-benefit ratio* was calculated in two ways. First, the cost-benefit ratio for sales improvement came to 225:1. Although this sounds spectacular, this refers to sales, not profits. Since this company's average profit margin was 8 percent, the cost-benefit ratio for increased profits was 18:1. That is, for every

(text continues on page 136)

Exhibit 7-2. Profit improvement model for hiring more productive salespeople.

---

1. SELECTION PROBLEM OR OPPORTUNITY

Opportunity: Potential to hire salespeople whose performance on the job approximates that of the company's top salespeople

2. COST OF SELECTION PROBLEM

Not Applicable
because this is an opportunity, not a problem

3. SOLUTION TO SELECTION PROBLEM OR OPPORTUNITY

An industrial psychologist conducted a concurrent validity study of the company's salespeople. This study resulted in a customized "success pattern" of scores that showed how the company's high-achiever salespeople tended to score on two tests:
  1. Test to predict on-the-job behavior
  2. Test to predict job-related mental abilities
Candidates for sales jobs took these two tests. The company then gave preference to hiring candidates who (a) scored similarly to the company's top salespeople and (b) did well on the company's traditional interviews and reference checks. Note: Previously hired salespeople were interviewed and reference-checked, but not tested.

4. COST OF SOLUTION

$4,000
Cost for concurrent validity study and for using the behavior and mental abilities tests for a year.

5. $ IMPROVEMENT BENEFIT

$900,000/year
(20 *new* salespeople hired *with tests* × *$255,000/year* in sales/new salesperson = $5,100,000/year.)

minus

(20 salespeople previously hired *without* tests × *$210,000/year* in sales/ previous salesperson = $4,200,000.)

=

$5,100,000/year − $4,200,000/year = $900,000/year.

(continues)

Exhibit 7-2   *(continued)*

---

6. COST/BENEFIT RATIO

18:1 in increased profits
$900,000:$4,000 in increased sales = 225:1 in increased sales
or, since company's average profit margin is 8%,
8% of 225:1 = 18:1 in increased profits.

$1 the company spent on its testing program, it reaped $18 in profits. Because the environment in which the company sold its products and its training methods remained basically unchanged during the period when both new and previous salespeople were hired, the profit improvement could be attributed in large part to the company using the two tests to help it hire the best—and avoid the rest.

Reducing Turnover Costs and Increasing Productivity

A precision machine shop company faced a serious *selection problem*. In a period of only two years, it had hired—and fired—thirteen machinists. Such employees are the backbone of the company's manufacturing operations and, as such, must have the skills required of first-rate machinists. They must do painstakingly exact calculations and calibrations.

The company evaluated machinist candidates only on the basis of interviews and reference checks. And as useful, valid reference checks became more difficult to obtain, it began relying almost exclusively on the interviews.

Unfortunately, the company's owner and managers continually got taken for a ride. Candidates for this job would "talk a good talk" and sound as if they knew what was involved in it. However, after they were hired, thirteen of the people who in the interview had sounded like first-rate machinists ended up performing on the job like third-rate machinists. That was the essential *selection problem* this company faced. The Six-Step Profit Improvement Model shown in Exhibit 7-3 summarizes how this organization overcame its profit-draining, business-depleting problem.

(text continues on page 138)

Exhibit 7-3. Profit improvement model for reducing turnover costs and improving productivity.

1. SELECTION PROBLEM OR OPPORTUNITY

Problem: A precision machine shop company had hired a number of technicians who did poor work that caused them to lose customers; they had to be terminated.

2. COST OF SELECTION PROBLEM

$390,845

Cost of selection problem = turnover costs per terminated machinist × number of terminated machinists = $30,015/terminated machinists × 13 terminated machinists = $390,195.

(See Exhibit 7–4 for turnover calculations, including lost business.)

3. SOLUTION TO SELECTION PROBLEM OR OPPORTUNITY

Work Simulation Test
(used as a key component of preemployment evaluations)

4. COST OF SOLUTION

$6,700

Cost included:

    A. Designing work simulation (to test candidates)

    B. Putting 52 candidates through work simulation (to hire 12 new machinists)

A. Designing work simulation = salary and benefits of company owner and managers while they designed work simulation and experimented with using it for one day = $1,500.

B. Putting 52 candidates through work simulation = cost to put 1 candidate through work simulation (mainly salary and benefits of company owner or a manager to administer the 2-hour simulation) × 52 candidates who were tested with the work simulation = $100/simulation × 52 simulations = $5,200.

5. $ IMPROVEMENT BENEFIT

$330,165

$ Improvement benefit = cost of turnover *before* company began using work simulation to hire 12 new machinists (i.e., Step 2: Cost of selection

(continues)

Exhibit 7-3   *(continued)*

---

problem) *minus* cost of turnover *after* company began using work simulation
= $390,195 − (2 turnovers × $30,015/turnover)
= $390,195 − $60,030 = $330,165.

6. COST-BENEFIT RATIO

49:1
$330,165:$6,700

The *cost of the selection problem* ended up being $390,195.
This consisted of the costs of turnover[3] for the thirteen terminated machinists. This turnover cost, laid out in Exhibit 7-4, included the following:

- Separation costs
- Replacement costs
- Training costs
- Lost productivity and business

The *solution to the selection problem* was to devise and use
a work simulation test. The company found out the hard (and
expensive) way that its machinist candidates could convince
interviewers that they could do the job. The managers who conducted the interviews were inexperienced and technically ill-
equipped to discern when candidates really knew how to do
what they claimed they could do on the job.

So, the company president and a foreman together designed a work simulation. In this work simulation, each candidate was required to carry out the make-or-break elements of
the job. The simulation took about two hours to administer to
each candidate. Either the company president or a manager observed each candidate and used a rating form to (1) record his
observations and (2) rate how well each job element was done.

Only candidates who received up arrows on the work simulation, the interviews, and (when possible) the reference check

(text continues on page 140)

Exhibit 7-4. Calculation of turnover costs.

Title of this job: **Machinist in Precision Machine Shop Company**

Turnover costs =
(A) separation costs + (B) replacement costs
+ (C) training costs + (D) lost productivity and business.

A. *SEPARATION COSTS*

1. Exit interview = cost of salary and benefits of both interviewer and departing employee during the exit interview = $15 + $15 = $30.
2. Administrative and record-keeping activities = $30.

Separation costs = $60.

B. *REPLACEMENT COSTS*

1. Advertising for job opening = $500.
2. Preemployment administrative functions and record keeping = $30.
3. Selection interviews = salary and benefits of managers and other interviewers while interviewing final candidates = $100.
4. Work simulations = $100.
5. Meetings to discuss candidates (salary and benefits of managers while participating in meetings) = $100.

Replacement costs = $830.

C. *TRAINING COSTS*

1. Booklets, manuals, and reports = $25.
2. Education (cost of workshops plus employee's salary and benefits while attending training) = $400.
3. One-on-one coaching = salary and benefits of both new employee and "coach," who is not fully productive while training new employee = $1,000.
4. Salary and benefits of new employee until he/she gets up to par (new employee's salary and benefits × number of days it should take a first-rate employee to get up to par) = $160/day × 20 days = $3,200.

Training costs = $4,625.

D. *LOST PRODUCTIVITY AND BUSINESS*

1. Lost productivity = average productivity lost because of mistakes and slow working pace of each terminated machinist = $14,500.

(continues)

Exhibit 7-4   *(continued)*

---

2. Lost customers = average annual amount of business of customers that stopped doing business with this company due to problems caused by the average terminated machinist = $10,000.
Lost productivity and business = $24,500.

$$TOTAL\ TURNOVER\ COSTS = \underset{A}{\$60} + \underset{B}{\$830} + \underset{C}{\$4,625} + \underset{D}{\$24,500}$$

$$= \$30,015$$
$$TOTAL^{\cdot}$$

---

were hired. The company estimated its *cost of solution* at about $100 for each work simulation it put an applicant through.

The $330,165 *$ improvement benefit* went straight to the company's bottom line. This third-of-a-million-dollar improvement resulted from hardly any new-hire machinists having to be terminated and the new machinists being highly productive and not losing business. The company's president also could have added as a benefit certain business contracts his company obtained owing to the excellent reputation his superb machinists helped create for the company's products. Interestingly, of the two machinists who were subsequently terminated, neither left because of inability to do the work. One quit to start his own business. And the other was fired for stealing from the company. A character test given to future machinist candidates should help prevent a recurrence of this problem (see Chapter 4).

Needless to say, the company president felt quite pleased with the 49:1 *cost-benefit ratio*. For every dollar plowed into the work simulation, the company reaped a $49 payback. Indeed, that was a very profitable investment.

Nonfinancial Rewards From Hiring High Achievers

Not all benefits from hiring good employees can be measured strictly in dollars and cents. Yet many bottom line improvements can probably be traced ultimately to hiring high achievers and avoiding underachievers.

What are some of the nonfinancial, nonquantifiable benefits of hiring productive, dependable, and honest employees. To begin with, hiring such praiseworthy employees results in managers experiencing *fewer:*

- Headaches (both the metaphorical and the physical kinds)
- Hours spent or wasted counseling or training below-average or merely average employees
- Troublemakers or "problem employees"
- Morale problems

At the same time, managers who hire the best have *more:*

- Motivated workers
- Employees able to acquire the knowledge and skills needed to do their jobs
- Productivity in ways that may be hard to measure quantitatively
- Espirit de corps among staff members who witness first-hand that the company seeks and expects excellence in its work force

Such nonfinancial rewards also have an impact on an organization's customers. These end-users of the company's products and services can tell the difference between dealing with top-notch employees and having to deal with average or only so-so workers. Their continued use of the organization may well depend on some of those unmeasurable, yet significant, characteristics that high-quality employees bring to work every day.

Benefits for Rejected Candidates When Companies Hire the Best

Almost all people have had jobs they wish they had never accepted. The work just does not fit with what they like to do. Or, the skills required seem excessively hard to learn. Or, the work seems boring or hateful. Or, the company's culture and ways of doing things feel uncomfortable. At some point, the dissatisfied person sits back and says, "I wish I had never been offered this job! And, above all, I wish I had never taken it."

Unfortunately, most people grapple with such realizations only after it is too late—after they are on the job. Since most managers do not do a good job at predicting which candidate will perform best on the job *and* fit into the organization's culture, such dilemmas occur all too often.

Fortunately, managers who interview, test, and reference check so that they hire only the best candidates for the job are actually offering rejected candidates a blessing in disguise. That occurs because *not* getting a job when it fails to coincide with a candidate's motivations, mental abilities, personality, or interpersonal style is an enormous benefit.

Sure, it feels terrible not to be chosen. But that upsetting or even embarrassing feeling soon passes. Other job opportunities will be found by anyone who possesses the requisite ambition, abilities, and persistence. So, it really is a lot better for an applicant to be rejected for a job after a valid, on-target evaluation than to take a job that later leads to feelings of distress, disappointment, and a dismal blemish on that person's career record.

Notes

1. Michael W. Mercer, *Turning Your Human Resources Department Into a Profit Center* (New York: AMACOM, 1989).
2. Michael W. Mercer, *Behavior Forecaster™ Test* (Chicago: Mercer Systems, Inc., 1991) and *Abilities Forecaster™ Test* (Chicago: Mercer Systems, Inc., 1991).
3. Wayne F. Cascio, *Costing Human Resources* (Boston: Kent, 1982), pp. 20–32; Michael W. Mercer, *Turning Your Human Resources Department Into a Profit Center*, p. 150; and Michael W. Mercer, "Turnover: Reducing The Costs," *Personnel*, December 1988, pp. 36–42.

8

Summary: Your Action Plan to Hire the Best— and Avoid the Rest

The *chief goal of evaluating a job candidate is to predict how success-fully or unsuccessfully that applicant will perform the job—before you put that person on the payroll.*

There are three main methods for making such predictions:

1. Interviews
2. Tests
3. Reference checks

Large-scale research studies indicate that thoroughly *validated tests provide the most accurate method of forecasting a candidate's on-the-job success.* By contrast, research also reveals that most predictions made on the basis of interviews prove about as useful as flipping a coin, and that most reference checks are as effective as simultaneously flipping a coin *and* rubbing a rabbit's foot for good luck.

However, to help you increase your chances of making accurate predictions on the basis of interviews and reference checks, earlier chapters provided structured ways of improving both methods. These techniques are explained and illustrated with numerous examples and ready-to-use materials.

Especially important, you must always keep in mind the

four essentials of useful and legally justifiable interviews, tests, and reference checks. Specifically, they must be:

1. Job-related
2. Valid
3. Reliable
4. Used by the organization in a nondiscriminatory manner

Another vital component of the prediction methods explained in this book is the use of a Candidate Rating Sheet. This sheet uses arrows pointing in three different directions to signify predictions as to how well a candidate will do with respect to the job-related criteria. The arrow ratings are as follows:

- ↑ = a positive rating
- → = an average rating
- ↓ = a negative rating

For example, the final Candidate Rating Sheet for our two hypothetical candidates, Terry Smith and Chris Jones, would look like Exhibit 8-1.

Remembering that all predictions as to a candidate's job success rely on the laws of probability, which candidate can you now predict is more likely to do well on the job—Terry or Chris? The candidate most likely to succeed is the candidate with all up arrows—or at least almost all up arrows.

Thus, Terry would probably do better than Chris. After all, every prediction of Terry's success—two interviews, two tests, a work simulation and a reference check—all point up. By contrast, Chris's ratings contain one negative and two average ratings. This makes Terry a safer bet than Chris when the hiring decision is made.

Checklist to Use in Planning How You'll Hire the Best

To help you keep all these prediction techniques in mind, you could benefit from an *easy-to-use checklist*. This action planning

Exhibit 8-1.   Candidate Rating Sheet filled out for two candidates, Terry Smith and Chris Jones.

	Terry Smith	Chris Jones
Interviewer #1	↑	↑
Interviewer #2	↑	↑
Test (*Behavior Forecaster*)	↑	↓
Test (*Abilities Forecaster*)	↑	↑
Work simulation (presentation)	↑	→
Reference check	↑	→

checklist, shown in Exhibit 8-2, provides a quick, ready reference that can help you jump start an organized strategy to *hire the best—and avoid the rest.*

By using this checklist and all the many other ready-to-use techniques presented in this book, you now are equipped to *hire the best—and avoid the rest.*

Exhibit 8-2.   Action plan checklist to hire the best.

Instructions
1. In the place provided, write the title of the job for which you want to hire a top-notch candidate.
2. Using checks and written answers, use this checklist to plan how you will evaluate candidates with a view to predicting their probability of succeeding in the job.

JOB TO BE FILLED: _____

Interviews

_____ List job-related criteria.
_____ Choose format for Interview Guide Form.
_____ Create customized Interview Guide Form to use in all interviews of candidates for this job.

List who will interview each candidate (fill in names):

1. _____
2. _____
3. _____

(continues)

Exhibit 8-2   *(continued)*

List date and hour when all interviewers will meet to discuss the candidates they have interviewed:

    Date: _____

    Time: _____

Location of meeting: _____

Tests

_____ Behavior Tests

    _____ Interpersonal skills
    _____ Personality traits
    _____ Motivations

_____ Mental Abilities Tests

    _____ Reasoning/problem-solving test
    _____ Vocabulary test
    _____ Grammar, spelling, and word use test
    _____ Arithmetic test
    _____ Small detail speed and accuracy test

_____ Character Tests

    _____ Trustworthiness
    _____ Commitment to work ethic
    _____ Substance abuse potential

_____ Technical Skills Tests

Fill in:

Technical Skills	*Test to Use*
A. _____	A. _____
B. _____	B. _____
C. _____	C. _____

_____ Work Simulations and Assessment Center Exercises

List simulations and exercises to use:

A. _____
B. _____
C. _____

_____ Evaluation of Executive Candidate

Name of industrial psychologist to do this executive
evaluation: _____

Reference Checks

_____ Over-the-Phone Reference Check
     _____ Create Reference Check Rating Form.
     _____ Call candidate's ex-bosses at work.
     _____ Call candidate's ex-bosses at home:
         _____ Weekday evening
         _____ Weekend
     _____ Talk to candidate's previous evening shift or night shift supervisors.
     _____ Talk to candidate's former secretaries.
List name of person who will do over-the-phone reference checks: _____

_____ Background Verification Reference Check
     _____ Previous employment
     _____ Criminal record
     _____ Credit history
     _____ Motor vehicle report
     _____ Academic history
     _____ Workers compensation claims
List person and/or reference checking agency that will do background verification reference checks: _____

Candidate Rating Sheet

List name of person who will create and fill in Candidate Rating Sheet on each candidate: _____

Appendixes

Appendix A. Sample of Interview Guide Form for Secretary Job

INTERVIEW GUIDE FORM
for
CANDIDATE FOR *SECRETARY*

CANDIDATE'S NAME: _____
INTERVIEWER'S NAME: _____
DATE OF INTERVIEW: _____

Job-Related Criteria	What to Look For	Notes	Rating
Friendliness	Likes being around people, makes good first impression, smiles, is outgoing		↓ → ↑
Persistence	Completes long-term projects, shows tenacity and stick-to-itiveness		↓ → ↑
Ability to follow rules and procedures	Works "by the book," follows established ways of doing tasks		↓ → ↑
Optimism	Focuses on solutions and opportunities rather than on problems or drawbacks; has a can-do attitude		↓ → ↑

Ability to handle stress	Is poised under pressure, does not mention feeling burned out or overloaded, has dry palms when shaking hands		↓ → ↑
Motivation to help people	Likes serving and assisting people, goes out of way to aid others, takes special interest in talking about helping people		↓ → ↑
Knowledge of computer programs: XYZ Word Processing and ABC Spreadsheet Programs	Knowledgeably discusses use of needed, or similar, word processing and spreadsheet programs		↓ → ↑
Organized Thinking	Is logical, systematic, uses lists, presents ideas in orderly fashion		↓ → ↑

Additional Observations and Notes:

OVERALL RATING OF THIS CANDIDATE: ↓ → ↑

Appendix B. Sample of Interview Guide Form for Manager Job

INTERVIEW GUIDE FORM
for
CANDIDATE FOR *MANAGER*

CANDIDATE'S NAME: _____

INTERVIEWER'S NAME: _____

DATE OF INTERVIEW: _____

Job-Related Criteria	*Positive Observations*	*Negative Observations*	*Rating*
Teamwork preference ___ Likes working in groups ___ Is collaborative ___ Dislikes working alone			↓ → ↑
Persuasiveness ___ Sways others' opinions and actions ___ Sells interviewer on self ___ Describes influencing others of diverse interpersonal styles			↓ → ↑ ↓ → ↑
Optimism ___ Focuses on solutions, not problems ___ Focuses on opportunities, not drawbacks ___ Shows can-do attitude ___ Enjoys overcoming obstacles			↓ → ↑

Power motivation			↓ → ↑
___ Enjoys taking charge			
___ Assumes control easily			
___ Exerts authority			
___ Has a take-charge spirit			
Planning ability			↓ → ↑
___ Makes plans for one or more years			
___ Sets priorities			
___ Lists action steps			
___ Sets deadlines for finishing each step			
Delegating and control-ling capacity			↓ → ↑
___ Assigns tasks to sub-ordinates			
___ Follows up on dele-gated work			
___ Inspects others' work in terms of —Quality —Quantity —Timeliness			
Ability to focus on de-tails			↓ → ↑
___ Spots trees, not just forest			
___ Tells "how to build clock, not just what time it is"			
___ Gives reasons for ac-tions without being asked why			

Ability to make objective decisions			↓ → ↑
___ Relies more on research than gut feelings			
___ Relies more on facts than intuition			
___ Researches possible outcomes before making decisions			
___ Does not let emotions get in way of decision			

OVERALL RATING OF THIS CANDIDATE: ↓ → ↑

Index